Math Contests
for
Grades 4, 5, and 6
Volume 1

School Years
1979-80 through 1985-86

Written by

Steven R. Conrad • Daniel Flegler

Published by MATH LEAGUE PRESS
Printed in the United States of America

Cover art by Bob DeRosa

Phil Frank Cartoons Copyright © 1993 by CMS

Third Printing, 1997

Math League Press
P.O. Box 720
Tenafly, NJ 07670-0720

ISBN 0-940805-06-5

Preface

Math Contests—Grades 4, 5 and 6, Volume 1 is the first volume in our series of problem books for grades 4, 5, and 6. This volume contains contests given in the school years 1979-80 through 1985-86, as well as three contests from the 1991-92 school year. The second and third volumes, which include separate contests for grades 4, 5, and 6, contain contests given from 1986-87 through 1995-96. (You can use the order form on page 94 to order any of our nine books.)

Seven of the ten contests in this book originally appeared in *The 1st Elementary Grades Math League Problem Book*, which is no longer published. These contests are included in this book because they have now been typeset and, more importantly, we now include complete solutions to *all* questions on all the contests.

We've divided this book into three sections for ease of use by students and teachers. The first section of the book contains the contests. Each contest is a 40-question multiple-choice contest that you can do in a 30-minute period. Each of the 3-page contests is designed so that questions on the 1st page are generally straightforward, those on the 2nd page are moderate in difficulty, and those on the 3rd page are more difficult. The second section of the book consists of detailed solutions to all the contest questions. The third and final section of the book consists of the letter answers to each contest and rating scales you can use to rate your performance.

Many people prefer to consult the answer section rather than the solution section when first reviewing a contest. We believe that reworking a problem when you know the answer (but *not* the solution) often leads to increased understanding of problem-solving techniques.

Until the 1988-89 school year, we offered a single contest known as the *Annual Elementary Grades Contest*. Before that time, any student in grade 6 or below was eligible to participate in this contest. Starting with the 1988-89 school year, we've sponsored three annual contests: the *Annual 4th Grade Contest*, the *Annual 5th Grade Contest*, and the *Annual 6th Grade Contest*. A student may participate in the contest designed for his/her current grade level, or for any higher grade level. For example, students in grades 4 and 5 (or below) are eligible to participate in the 6th Grade Contest.

Steven R. Conrad & Daniel Flegler, contest authors

i

Acknowledgments

For her continued patience and understanding, special thanks to Marina Conrad, whose only mathematical skill, an important one, is the ability to count the ways.

For her lifetime support and encouragement, special thanks to Mildred Flegler.

To Alan Feldman, who proofread this book, thanks!

Table Of Contents

The Contests

• •

1979-80 through 1985-86

1979-80 Elementary Grades Contest

for students in grades 5 & 6

Instructions

- **Time** You will have only *30 minutes* working time for this contest. You might be *unable* to finish all 40 questions in the time allowed.

- **Scores** Please remember that *this is a contest, not a test*—and there is no "passing" or "failing" score. Few students score as high as 30 points (75% correct). Students with half that, 15 points, *deserve commendation!*

- **Format and Point Value** This is a multiple-choice contest. Every answer is an A, B, C, or D. For each question, write your answer in the *Answers* column to the right of the question. A correct answer is worth 1 point. Unanswered questions get no credit.

1. There are 10 chickens and 10 cows. How many legs are there?   1.
    A) 20   B) 40   C) 60   D) 80

2. $\frac{5075}{25} =$ 2.

    A) 23   B) 203   C) 213   D) 230

3. If a radius of circle is 8 cm long, how long is a diameter?   3.
    A) 4 cm   B) 8 cm   C) 16 cm   D) 64 cm

4. $2.7 - 1.8 =$ 4.
    A) 4.5   B) 1.9   C) 1.1   D) 0.9

5. Find the number of dots shown   . . . .   5.
                                             . . . .
    in the drawing at the right.   . . . .
                                             . . . .
    A) 28   B) 32   C) 48   D) 60

6. $42 \times 79 - 79 \times 42 =$ 6.
    A) 0   B) 1659   C) 3318   D) 6636

7. Round 1849 to the nearest hundred.   7.
    A) 1800   B) 1850   C) 1900   D) 2000

8. $\frac{2 \times 2 \times 2 \times 2}{2 + 2 + 2 + 2}$ 8.

    A) 0   B) 1   C) 2   D) 4

9. Find the greatest common factor of 12 and 18.   9.
    A) 6   B) 12   C) 18   D) 36

10. $10 - 9 + 8 - 7 + 6 - 5 + 4 - 3 + 2 - 1 =$ 10.
    A) 45   B) 5   C) 4   D) 1

11. Find the number of quarters in 8 dollars.   11.
    A) 2   B) 4   C) 16   D) 32

12. Chris bought items that cost $1.21, $2.57, and $1.94. How much   12.
    change should Chris receive when paying with a $10 bill?
    A) $5.72   B) $5.28   C) $4.72   D) $4.28

13. 13 thousands + 13 hundreds + 13 ones   13.
    A) 1313   B) 14313   C) 14413   D) 131313

14. Find the least common multiple of 4 and 10.   14.
    A) 2   B) 14   C) 20   D) 40

15. $12\frac{1}{2}\%$ of 80 =   15.

    A) 10   B) 12   C) 16   D) 100

Go on to the next page ⇨ **E**

2

	Answers
16. Mary has 41¢ in coins. No two coins have the same value. How many coins does Mary have? A) 4 B) 5 C) 6 D) 7	16.
17. $12 \times 57 + 12 \times 43 =$ A) 2400 B) 1298 C) 1296 D) 1200	17.
18. A man needs six pieces of wire, each 218 centimeters long. Wire is sold only by the meter. How many meters of wire must the man buy? A) 13 B) 14 C) 18 D) 1308	18.
19. $2.25 \times 0.80 =$ A) $1\frac{1}{2}$ B) $1\frac{3}{4}$ C) $1\frac{4}{5}$ D) 2	19.
20. How many 2's must be multiplied together for the product to be a number between 100 and 200? A) 51 B) 7 C) 6 D) 5	20.
21. $5 \times 1000 + 7 \times 100 + 3 \times 1 =$ A) 573 B) 5073 C) 5703 D) 5730	21.
22. Find the missing number: 2:3 as _?_ :15. A) 9 B) 10 C) 14 D) 16	22.
23. Find the average of 0.3, 0.03, and 0.003. A) 0.111 B) 0.333 C) 0.666 D) 0.999	23.
24. Which of the following is *not* a prime number? A) 41 B) 51 C) 61 D) 71	24.
25. The next number in the sequence 1, 3, 7, 13, 21, . . . is A) 37 B) 35 C) 33 D) 31	25.
26. Two circles and one straight line are drawn. Find the largest possible number of intersection points for this drawing. A) 2 B) 4 C) 6 D) 8	26.
27. Find the missing number: $\frac{44 \times 55}{?} = 4 \times 5$. A) 11 B) 22 C) 45 D) 121	27.
28. On a $\frac{1}{2}$ hour TV program, commercials were shown for 5 minutes. For what fractional part of the $\frac{1}{2}$ hour were commercials shown? A) $\frac{1}{5}$ B) $\frac{1}{6}$ C) $\frac{1}{10}$ D) $\frac{1}{12}$	28.
29. Which of the following fractions is less than one-third? A) $\frac{5}{14}$ B) $\frac{15}{46}$ C) $\frac{31}{90}$ D) $\frac{104}{309}$	29.

Go on to the next page ⫸ **E**

3

30. In Dracsylvania, people use DRACS instead of dollars, and 1 DRAC equals $1.70. For these people, $34.00 =

   A) 2 DRACS   B) 17 DRACS   C) 20 DRACS   D) 34 DRACS | 30.

31. $6^2 + 8^2 =$

   A) 7^2 B) 10^2 C) 14^2 D) 28^2 | 31.

32. Find the number of seconds in 3.5 hours.

   A) 210   B) 3600   C) 10800   D) 12600 | 32.

33. Danny was supposed to multiply a number by 5. By mistake, he divided the number by 5 instead. Danny's answer was 5. The correct answer was

   A) 1   B) 25   C) 50   D) 125 | 33.

34. If 18 people share a barrel of apples equally, each gets 12 apples. If there had been 6 fewer people, how many apples would each person have gotten?

   A) 6   B) 9   C) 18   D) 36 | 34.

35. In a class of 30 students, exactly 7 have tape recorders, exactly 15 have pocket calculators, and exactly 2 have both. How many of the 30 students have neither?

   A) 10   B) 8   C) 6   D) 4 | 35.

36. $\dfrac{1}{2 + \dfrac{1}{2 + \dfrac{1}{2}}} =$

   A) $\frac{1}{3}$ B) $\frac{2}{5}$ C) $\frac{2}{9}$ D) $\frac{5}{12}$ | 36.

37. A rectangular lot 30 m by 40 m is surrounded on all 4 sides by a concrete walk 5 m wide. Find the area of the surface of the walk.

   A) 800 m^2 B) 700 m^2 C) 375 m^2 D) 350 m^2 | 37.

38. There are four identical pieces of chain, each three links long. It cost 5¢ to open a link and 6¢ to close one. The least it costs to join all twelve links into a single "circle" is

   A) 22¢   B) 33¢   C) 44¢   D) 88¢ | 38.

39. The average of six consecutive whole numbers could be

   A) $36\frac{1}{3}$ B) $44\frac{1}{6}$ C) $48\frac{1}{2}$ D) 54 | 39.

40. In the diagram ⊟, three rectangles are pictured—two small ones and one larger one. How many rectangles are pictured in ⊞?

   A) 7   B) 9   C) 16   D) 18 | 40.

The end of the contest 🖎 **E**

Solutions on Page 41 · Answers on Page 82

4

ELEMENTARY GRADES MATHEMATICS CONTEST

Math League Press, P.O. Box 720, Tenafly, New Jersey 07670

1980-81 Elementary Grades Contest
for students in grades 5 & 6

Instructions

- **Time** You will have only *30 minutes* working time for this contest. You might be *unable* to finish all 40 questions in the time allowed.

- **Scores** Please remember that *this is a contest, not a test*—and there is no "passing" or "failing" score. Few students score as high as 30 points (75% correct). Students with half that, 15 points, *deserve commendation!*

- **Format and Point Value** This is a multiple-choice contest. Every answer is an A, B, C, or D. For each question, write your answer in the *Answers* column to the right of the question. A correct answer is worth 1 point. Unanswered questions get no credit.

1. The largest whole number less than 1000 is A) 99 B) 990 C) 999 D) 999.9	1.
2. $148 + 149 + 150 + 151 + 152 =$ A) 740 B) 750 C) 760 D) 770	2.
3. Which is equal to 3? A) $\frac{3}{3}$ B) $\frac{6}{3}$ C) $\frac{9}{3}$ D) $\frac{12}{3}$	3.
4. $5 \times 4 \times 3 \times 2 \times 1 \times 0 =$ A) 0 B) 15 C) 120 D) 1200	4.
5. A rectangle has a length of 8 cm and a width of 5 cm. Find the perimeter of the rectangle. A) 13 cm B) 26 cm C) 40 cm D) 80 cm	5.
6. A baseball team won 4 games and lost 20. What fraction of its games did the team win? A) $\frac{1}{5}$ B) $\frac{1}{4}$ C) $\frac{4}{5}$ D) $\frac{1}{6}$	6.
7. $\frac{3 \times 4 \times 5 \times 6 \times 7}{7 \times 6 \times 5 \times 4 \times 3} =$ A) 0 B) 0.2520 C) 1 D) 2520	7.
8. $\frac{0}{10} =$ A) 0.10 B) 1 C) 0.1 D) 0	8.
9. $10 \times 100 \times 1000 =$ A) 1 000 000 B) 11 000 000 C) 100 000 000 D) 111 000 000	9.
10. $6 \times \frac{1}{2} \times \frac{1}{3}$ has the same value as A) $6 + 6$ B) $6 - 6$ C) 6×6 D) $\frac{6}{6}$	10.
11. The perimeter of an equilateral triangle is 24 cm. The length of one side of this triangle is A) 8 cm B) 12 cm C) 16 cm D) 72 cm	11.
12. $\frac{32}{48}$ A) $\frac{2}{3}$ B) $\frac{3}{4}$ C) $\frac{5}{6}$ D) $\frac{11}{12}$	12.
13. $0.91 + 0.19 =$ A) 1.9 B) 1.1 C) 1.01 D) 1	13.
14. Of the following, which is the largest? A) 2.2 B) 2.02 C) 2.002 D) 2.00	14.
15. How many hundreds are there in 1 000 000? A) 1 million B) 1 thousand C) 10 thousand D) 100 thousand	15.

Go on to the next page ▐▐▐▶ **E**

16. $\frac{1}{10} + \frac{2}{10} + \frac{3}{10} + \frac{4}{10} =$

    A) $\frac{1}{4}$ B) $\frac{1}{2}$ C) $\frac{9}{10}$ D) 1

    16.

17. Find the missing number: $1000 \times 968 = 10 \times \underline{\ ?\ }$

    A) 0.968   B) 9.68   C) 96 800   D) 968 000

    17.

18. 0.1 + 0.3 + 0.5 + 0.7 + 0.9 has the same value as

    A) 6×0.6 B) 5×0.5 C) 4×0.4 D) 3×0.3

    18.

19. $33\frac{1}{3}\%$ of 90 is

    A) 18   B) 27   C) 30   D) 45

    19.

20. The scale of a map is: $\frac{3}{4}$ of an inch = 10 miles. If the distance on the map between two towns is 12 inches, the actual distance between the towns is

    A) 90 miles   B) 120 miles   C) 150 miles   D) 160 miles

    20.

21. Which number leaves a remainder of 1 when divided by 5 and also when divided by 7?

    A) 153   B) 315   C) 351   D) 531

    21.

22. Which of the following numbers is divisible by 3?

    A) 11 111   B) 1 111 111   C) 11 111 111   D) 111 111 111

    22.

23. Sue had an average of exactly 84 after taking two tests. On the third test she scored 96. Find her average for all three tests.

    A) 88   B) 90   C) 91   D) 92

    23.

24. Find the missing number: $\frac{20}{32} = \frac{?}{24}$.

    A) 15   B) 16   C) 17   D) 18

    24.

25. In the number 987 654 321 000, what digit is in the ten millions' place?

    A) 4   B) 5   C) 6   D) 7

    25.

26. How many prime numbers are there between 20 and 30?

    A) 1   B) 2   C) 3   D) 4

    26.

27. $\frac{1}{4} + 0.75 =$

    A) 0.775   B) 0.95   C) 0.975   D) 1

    27.

28. There is a balance scale. On one side is put a full brick. On the other side is put both a half-brick and a 6 lb. weight. Both sides now weigh the same. Find the weight of the full brick.

    A) 3 lbs.   B) 6 lbs.   C) 9 lbs.   D) 12 lbs.

    28.

29. $\frac{1}{2}\% =$

    A) 0.5   B) 0.05   C) 0.005   D) 0.0005

    29.

Go on to the next page ⏵ **E**

30. How many whole numbers from 1 to 100 contain the digit 2 exactly once? A) 9 B) 18 C) 19 D) 20	30.
31. The largest whole number divisor of 2468 which is less than 2468 is A) 2467 B) 1234 C) 842 D) 617	31.
32. The next number in the sequence 1, 1, 2, 3, 5, 8, 13, . . . is A) 21 B) 20 C) 19 D) 15	32.
33. Which of the following fractions is between $\frac{1}{3}$ and $\frac{1}{4}$? A) $\frac{2}{5}$ B) $\frac{2}{7}$ C) $\frac{2}{9}$ D) $\frac{2}{11}$	33.
34. The Hulk is 3 cm taller than Tarzan and 4 cm shorter than Superman. If Superman's height is 2 meters, then Tarzan's height is A) 193 cm B) 197 cm C) 203 cm D) 207 cm	34.
35. $\dfrac{1}{\frac{1}{2}} + \dfrac{1}{\frac{1}{3}} =$ A) $\frac{5}{6}$ B) $\frac{5}{3}$ C) $\frac{12}{5}$ D) 5	35.
36. All angles in the figure are right angles. The perimeter of the figure is between A) 15 and 26 B) 37 and 44 C) 45 and 55 D) 100 and 200	36.
37. If 5% of a certain number is 16, then 25% of half the number is A) 2 B) 4 C) 40 D) 80	37.
38. A *palindrome* is any word or number which reads the same forwards or backwards. For example, the number "12321" and the word "level" are both palindromes. How many whole numbers between 100 and 1000 are palindromes? A) 9 B) 81 C) 90 D) 99	38.
39. Which can be written as the product of three even numbers? A) 166 B) 168 C) 170 D) 172	39.
40. A clock that uniformly loses 4 minutes every 24 hours was correctly set at 6 A.M. on January 1. What was the time indicated by this clock when the correct time was 12 o'clock noon on January 6 of the same year? A) 11:36 A.M. B) 11:38 A.M. C) 11:39 A.M. D) 11:40 A.M.	40.

The end of the contest 🖎 **E**

Solutions on Page 45 · Answers on Page 83

ELEMENTARY GRADES MATHEMATICS CONTEST

Math League Press, P.O. Box 720, Tenafly, New Jersey 07670

1981-82 Elementary Grades Contest
for students in grades 5 & 6

Instructions

- **Time** You will have only *30 minutes* working time for this contest. You might be *unable* to finish all 40 questions in the time allowed.

- **Scores** Please remember that *this is a contest, not a test*—and there is no "passing" or "failing" score. Few students score as high as 30 points (75% correct). Students with half that, 15 points, *deserve commendation!*

- **Format and Point Value** This is a multiple-choice contest. Every answer is an A, B, C, or D. For each question, write your answer in the *Answers* column to the right of the question. A correct answer is worth 1 point. Unanswered questions get no credit.

Answers

1. $9999 + 2 =$ A) 10001 B) 10011 C) 10101 D) 11111	1.
2. In a 400-page book, each chapter has approximately 20 pages. Approximately how many chapters does this book have? A) 20 B) 40 C) 80 D) 8000	2.
3. $1982 - 1892 =$ A) 190 B) 170 C) 90 D) 70	3.
4. $\dfrac{1+2+3}{3+4+5} =$ A) $\dfrac{43}{50}$ B) $\dfrac{1}{2}$ C) $\dfrac{1}{8}$ D) $\dfrac{1}{3}$	4.
5. One soft drink cost 60¢ and one hamburger costs 75¢. Ten soft drinks and four hamburgers cost A) \$9 B) \$10 C) \$11 D) \$12	5.
6. When 6 is divided by $\frac{1}{2}$, the result is A) $\dfrac{1}{12}$ B) $\dfrac{1}{3}$ C) 3 D) 12	6.
7. $(29 + 30) + 31 =$ A) $29 + (30 + 31)$ B) $29 \times (30 + 31)$ C) $(29 + 31) + (30 + 31)$ D) $(29 \times 31) + (30 \times 31)$	7.
8. When 112 is divided by 12, the remainder is A) 1 B) 2 C) 3 D) 4	8.
9. Find the missing number: $\dfrac{2}{11} + \dfrac{1}{22} + \dfrac{0}{33} = \dfrac{?}{44}$. A) 0 B) 3 C) 6 D) 10	9.
10. $(4 \times 1000) + (7 \times 100) + (9 \times 1) =$ A) 4790 B) 4709 C) 4079 D) 479	10.
11. Find the largest number that leaves a remainder of 10 when divided into 90. A) 20 B) 40 C) 80 D) 100	11.
12. $88\overline{)888888} =$ A) 11111 B) 10101 C) 10001 D) 111	12.
13. Find the greatest common factor of 7 and 9. A) 1 B) 7 C) 9 D) 63	13.
14. $(7 \times 87) + (3 \times 87) =$ A) 860 B) 870 C) 880 D) 890	14.
15. Find the area of a square each of whose sides is 3 cm long. A) 6 sq. cm B) 9 sq. cm C) 12 sq. cm D) 81 sq. cm	15.

Go on to the next page ⫸ **E**

	Answers
16. $\frac{19}{3} =$ A) $4\frac{1}{3}$ B) $5\frac{1}{3}$ C) $6\frac{1}{3}$ D) 16	16.
17. Which of the following numbers is the largest? A) $\frac{1}{1981}$ B) $\frac{1982}{1983}$ C) $\frac{1981}{1982}$ D) $\frac{1981}{1984}$	17.
18. In Paris, a boy walks 4 km north, 5 km south, 2 km north, and 3 km south. How far is the boy from his starting point? A) 14 km north B) 14 km south C) 2 km north D) 2 km south	18.
19. Find the number of seconds in one hour. A) 60 B) 360 C) 3 600 D) 216 000	19.
20. The value of $\frac{1}{2} \times \frac{2}{3} \times \frac{3}{4} \times \frac{4}{5} \times \frac{5}{6} \times \frac{6}{7} \times \frac{7}{8} \times \frac{8}{9}$ is A) $\frac{1}{9}$ B) $\frac{3}{8}$ C) $\frac{856}{1279}$ D) $\frac{12345678}{23456789}$	20.
21. The area of a rectangle is 24 sq. cm. The length of one side of the rectangle is 8 cm. The perimeter of the rectangle is A) 3 cm B) 11 cm C) 22 cm D) 24 cm	21.
22. $0.1 - 0.01 =$ A) 0 B) 0.09 C) 0.11 D) 0.99	22.
23. The fraction $\frac{2}{3}$ keeps the same value when both its numerator and denominator are A) multiplied by 2 B) increased by 2 C) decreased by 2 D) squared	23.
24. 20% of 20 = A) $\frac{1}{4}$ B) $\frac{1}{5}$ C) 0.4 D) 4	24.
25. The sum of the measures of the two smallest angles of a right triangle is A) 45° B) 90° C) 180° D) 360°	25.
26. $3\frac{4}{25} =$ A) 3.8 B) 3.4 C) 3.16 D) 3.04	26.
27. The number of nickels in $1 is the same as the number of quarters in A) $4 B) $5 C) $20 D) $100	27.
28. Which of the following is equal to one million? A) one hundred thousands B) ten thousands C) one hundred hundreds D) one thousand thousands	28.
29. Adding 3 to a certain number gives the same result as multiplying that certain number by 2. The number is A) 2 B) 3 C) 5 D) 6	29.

Go on to the next page ⮞ **E**

30. The length of one side of a regular hexagon is 30 cm. What is the perimeter of the hexagon? A) 5 cm B) 6 cm C) 150 cm D) 180 cm	30.
31. Which one of the following numbers is *not* a multiple of 3? A) 123 123 B) 223 223 C) 423 423 D) 723 723	31.
32. $4 \times 4 \times 4 \times 4 \times 4 =$ A) 5^4 B) 4×5 C) 4^4 D) 2^{10}	32.
33. In the number 110 000, the place-value of the left-most "1" minus the place-value of the right-most "1" is A) 10 B) 100 C) 90 000 D) 100 000	33.
34. Dale sold an entire roll of consecutively numbered tickets. The number on the first ticket was 1982. The number on the last ticket was 2132. How many tickets did Dale sell? A) 149 B) 150 C) 151 D) 250	34.
35. The average of three numbers is 20. Suppose that the first number is increased by 1, the second number is increased by 2, and the third number is increased by 3. The average of the three numbers has been increased by A) 1 B) 2 C) 3 D) 6	35.
36. After a girl spends $\frac{1}{3}$ of her money and loses $\frac{1}{2}$ of the remainder, she then has $10 left. She started with A) $30 B) $45 C) $50 D) $60	36.
37. In a class, the ratio of the number of boys to the number of girls is 2 to 3. The number of boys is what per cent of the number of students in the entire class? A) 20% B) 40% C) 60% D) $66\frac{2}{3}$%	37.
38. If 60 meters of uniform wire weighs 80 grams, what is the weight of 141 meters of this wire? A) 160 grams B) 162 grams C) 165 grams D) 188 grams	38.
39. The numbers 1, 2, 3, 4, 5, 6, 7, 8, 9, 10, 11, and 12 are arranged in 3 columns of 4 numbers each so that the sum of the numbers in each column is the same. The sum of the numbers in each column is A) 18 B) 21 C) 26 D) 32	39.
40. In an *upside-down year*, each digit can be turned upside down to form a new year. For example, 1981 is an *upside-down year* since it becomes 1681 when each digit is turned upside down. Between 1982 and 2000, how many *upside-down years* are there? A) 6 B) 7 C) 8 D) 9	40.

The end of the contest ✍ **E**

Solutions on Page 49 · Answers on Page 84

1982-83 Elementary Grades Contest

for students in grades 5 & 6

Instructions

- **Time** You will have only *30 minutes* working time for this contest. You might be *unable* to finish all 40 questions in the time allowed.

- **Scores** Please remember that *this is a contest, not a test*—and there is no "passing" or "failing" score. Few students score as high as 30 points (75% correct). Students with half that, 15 points, *deserve commendation!*

- **Format and Point Value** This is a multiple-choice contest. Every answer is an A, B, C, or D. For each question, write your answer in the *Answers* column to the right of the question. A correct answer is worth 1 point. Unanswered questions get no credit.

Answers

1. $(1 + 9 + 8 + 3) - (3 + 8 + 9 + 1) =$
   A) 0   B) 1   C) 2   D) 3

   1.

2. $98 + 98 + 98 + 98 + 98 + 98 + 98 + 98 + 98 + 98 =$
   A) 962   B) 970   C) 972   D) 980

   2.

3. Which is equal to 4?
   A) $\frac{44}{4}$ B) $\frac{4 \times 4}{4}$ C) $44 - 4$ D) $(4 \times 4) - 4$

   3.

4. $2 \times 3 \times 4 \times 5 =$
   A) 6×20 B) $2 \times 10 \times 12$ C) $6 \times 8 \times 10$ D) $6 \times 4 \times 6 \times 5$

   4.

5. $(27 + 29) + (73 + 71) =$
   A) 100   B) 180   C) 200   D) 220

   5.

6. How many prime numbers are there between 0 and 10?
   A) 3   B) 4   C) 5   D) 6

   6.

7. $\frac{1}{9} + \frac{3}{9} + \frac{5}{9} =$
   A) $\frac{1}{3}$ B) 1   C) $\frac{10}{9}$ D) $\frac{5}{243}$

   7.

8. A car left New York at 9:00 A.M. on Tuesday and arrived in Toronto at 1:00 P.M. on Wednesday. This trip took
   A) 4 hours   B) 16 hours   C) 24 hours   D) 28 hours

   8.

9. $2 \times \frac{1}{2} \times 2 \times \frac{1}{2} \times 2 =$
   A) 4   B) 2   C) 1   D) $\frac{1}{2}$

   9.

10. The average of 74, 76, and 81 is
    A) 75   B) 76   C) 77   D) 78

    10.

11. Which of the following is *not* a polygon?
    A) triangle   B) rhombus   C) square   D) circle

    11.

12. Chris left school and walked 2 km east, then 3 km west, then 4 km east, then 2 km west, and finally, 6 km east. How many kilometers away from school is Chris now?
    A) 0   B) 7   C) 10   D) 17

    12.

13. Which of the following numbers has 3 as a factor?
    A) 1981   B) 1982   C) 1983   D) 1984

    13.

14. $0.2 \times 0.5 =$
    A) 1   B) 0.1   C) 0.01   D) 0.001

    14.

15. $5 + (10 \times 8) + (100 \times 9) + (1000 \times 2) =$
    A) 5892   B) 5111   C) 1115   D) 2985

    15.

16. Find the largest whole number such that 6 times that number is less than 100.
    A) 15   B) 16   C) 17   D) 95

    16.

Go on to the next page ▥➡ **E**

17. 4 cm =
    A) 400 m   B) 40 m   C) 0.4 m   D) 0.04 m

18. The sum of the digits of 7472 is 7 + 4 + 7 + 2 or 20. The sum of the digits of 99 999 999 999 999 999 999 is
    A) 20   B) 171   C) 180   D) 999

19. 0.1919 + 0.9191 =
    A) 1   B) 1.1   C) 1.11   D) 1.111

20. The perimeter of a rectangle is 48 cm. The length of the rectangle is 16 cm. The width of the rectangle is
    A) 3 cm   B) 8 cm   C) 16 cm   D) 32 cm

21. $8\overline{)16161616}$ =
    A) 2222   B) 20222   C) 202022   D) 2020202

22. There are twice as many boys in a room as girls. If 5 boys leave the room, there would be an equal number of boys and girls in the room. How many boys were in the room at first?
    A) 5   B) 10   C) 15   D) 20

23. $12\times(\frac{1}{2} + \frac{1}{3} + \frac{1}{4})$ =
    A) 72   B) 13   C) $\frac{4}{3}$ D) $\frac{1}{2}$

24. $12\times(\frac{1}{2} \times \frac{1}{3} \times \frac{1}{4})$ =
    A) 72   B) 13   C) $\frac{4}{3}$ D) $\frac{1}{2}$

25. The area of each of the 9 small squares is 9. The perimeter of the largest square is
    A) 12   B) 36   C) 81   D) 108

26. 50% of 50% of 50% of 100% is
    A) 125%   B) 12.5%   C) 1.25%   D) 0.125%

27. On the planet Strangus, there are 15 months in a year, 7 weeks in a month, and 5 days in a week. A Strangus year has
    A) 27 days   B) 425 days   C) 525 days   D) 625 days

28. A genius reads 100 words backwards per second. How long does it take her to read 31 000 words backwards?
    A) 5 minutes, 10 seconds   B) 5 minutes, 30 seconds
    C) 5 minutes, 20 seconds   D) 5 minutes, 40 seconds

29. From 6 days 7 hours 35 minutes subtract 3 days 9 hours 50 minutes.
    A) 2 days 22 hours 45 minutes   B) 2 days 21 hours 45 minutes
    C) 2 days 7 hours 15 minutes   D) 2 days 2 hours 15 minutes

Go on to the next page ⫸ **E**

---

30. The length of a radius of a circle is 20 cm. A line segment is drawn between two points on the circle. The length of this line segment *cannot* be

    A) 50 cm   B) 40 cm   C) 2 cm   D) 1 cm

30.

---

31. A man has 10 sons. Each of these sons has 10 sons. How many people does that make all together?

    A) 21   B) 100   C) 101   D) 111

31.

---

32. If 5 apples cost the same as 4 oranges, find the ratio of the cost of 1 apple to the cost of 1 orange.

    A) 5:9   B) 4:9   C) 5:4   D) 4:5

32.

---

33. Find the missing number: $\frac{?}{17} = \frac{1}{2}$.

    A) 8.5   B) 1.7   C) 17   D) 34

33.

---

34. What is the minimum number of arrows that must be turned in some manner so that all the arrows point in the same direction?

    A) 4   B) 5   C) 6   D) 11

34.

---

35. A year is called a *Blackjack* year if the sum of its digits is 21. For example, 1983 is a *Blackjack* year since $1 + 9 + 8 + 3 = 21$. How many *Blackjack* years are there between 1900 and 2000?

    A) 10   B) 9   C) 8   D) 7

35.

---

36. Which of the following fractions has the greatest value?

    A) $\frac{51}{100}$ B) $\frac{152}{300}$ C) $\frac{52}{103}$ D) $\frac{50}{99}$

36.

---

37. Joan bought a painting for $10, sold it for $20, repurchased it for $30, then resold it for $40. Joan

    A) broke even   B) made $20   C) lost $10   D) lost $20

37.

---

38. If a chicken lays one egg in one minute, how many minutes does it take 3 chickens to lay a total of 3 eggs?

    A) $\frac{1}{3}$ B) 1   C) 3   D) 9

38.

---

39. By what fractional part of $\frac{4}{5}$ does $\frac{3}{5}$ exceed $\frac{2}{5}$?

    A) $\frac{1}{5}$ B) $\frac{1}{4}$ C) $\frac{2}{5}$ D) $\frac{3}{5}$

39.

---

40. Find the missing number:
$2 + 4 + 6 + \ldots + 1984 = (1 + 3 + 5 + \ldots + 1983) + \underline{?}$

    A) 992   B) 1984   C) 1985   D) 3968

40.

The end of the contest 🖎 **E**

Solutions on Page 53 · Answers on Page 85

1983-84 Elementary Grades Contest

for students in grades 5 & 6

Instructions

- **Time** You will have only *30 minutes* working time for this contest. You might be *unable* to finish all 40 questions in the time allowed.

- **Scores** Please remember that *this is a contest, not a test*—and there is no "passing" or "failing" score. Few students score as high as 30 points (75% correct). Students with half that, 15 points, *deserve commendation!*

- **Format and Point Value** This is a multiple-choice contest. Every answer is an A, B, C, or D. For each question, write your answer in the *Answers* column to the right of the question. A correct answer is worth 1 point. Unanswered questions get no credit.

1. Which has a value different from 1984?
   A) $1984 + 0$ B) 1984×1 C) $1984 \div 1$ D) $1984 + 1$

   1.

2. $\frac{13}{13} + \frac{15}{15} + \frac{17}{17} + \frac{19}{19} =$

   A) 1   B) $\frac{66}{19}$ C) 2   D) 4

   2.

3. The sum of an odd number and an even number is always
   A) an odd number   B) an even number
   C) a prime number   D) a multiple of 3

   3.

4. 111 111 111 divided by 9 equals
   A) 12 345 678   B) 12 345 679   C) 123 456 789   D) 123 456 799

   4.

5. $1 000 000 - 101 =$
   A) 999 999   B) 999 989   C) 999 899   D) 999 889

   5.

6. Which is the largest number?
   A) $\frac{4}{5}$ B) $\frac{5}{6}$ C) $\frac{2}{3}$ D) $\frac{3}{4}$

   6.

7. $32 123 + 12 321 =$
   A) 44 444   B) 54 444   C) 55 555   D) 45 454

   7.

8. In which number does the digit 2 represent 200?
   A) 1423   B) 2134   C) 1234   D) 4132

   8.

9. $9998 + 9999 + 10000 + 10001 + 10002 =$
   A) 49998   B) 49999   C) 50000   D) 50001

   9.

10. $\frac{7}{6} + \frac{8}{6} + \frac{9}{6} =$
    A) 5   B) 4   C) 3   D) 2

    10.

11. $(876 \times 543) - (543 \times 876) =$
    A) 0   B) 1   C) 237 834   D) 475 668

    11.

12. Find the sum of the measures of all three angles of a right triangle.
    A) 90°   B) 150°   C) 180°   D) 360°

    12.

13. $0.33 =$
    A) $\frac{3}{10}$ B) $\frac{33}{100}$ C) $\frac{1}{3}$ D) $\frac{3}{8}$

    13.

14. There are 30 students in a class, and three-fifths of them are girls. How many *boys* are in the class?
    A) 6   B) 12   C) 18   D) 24

    14.

15. 20 divided by $\frac{1}{2}$ equals
    A) 40   B) 10   C) 5   D) 2

    15.

Go on to the next page ⫸ **E**

16. How many whole numbers leave no remainder when divided into 60?
    A) 10　　　　B) 12　　　　C) 15　　　　D) 30

17. $\dfrac{1 + 2 + 3 + 4 + 5}{1 \times 2 \times 3 \times 4 \times 5} =$
    A) 0　　　　B) $\frac{1}{8}$　　　　C) 1　　　　D) 8

18. The largest prime factor of 1984 is
    A) 23　　　　B) 29　　　　C) 31　　　　D) 64

19. The number of minutes in 4 hours is the same as the number of hours in
    A) 4 days　　B) 6 days　　C) 10 days　　D) 60 days

20. Find the missing number: $23 \times \underline{\ ?\ } = 1081$.
    A) 43　　　　B) 47　　　　C) 57　　　　D) 1058

21. In multiplying a number by $\frac{1}{100}$, the result may be obtained by moving the decimal point of that number
    A) two places to the left　　　　B) one place to the left
    C) two places to the right　　　　D) one place to the right

22. The least common multiple of 12, 18, and 30 is
    A) 6　　　　B) 60　　　　C) 180　　　　D) 540

23. $1\frac{2}{3} + 2\frac{1}{2} =$
    A) $3\frac{3}{5}$　　　　B) $3\frac{5}{6}$　　　　C) $4\frac{1}{6}$　　　　D) $4\frac{1}{3}$

24. If a diameter of a circle is 20, then a radius of this circle is
    A) 40　　　　B) 40π　　　　C) 10　　　　D) 10π

25. $\dfrac{6666}{33} =$
    A) 2222　　　B) 2020　　　C) 222　　　D) 202

26. Which number is closer to 473 than it is to 449?
    A) 455　　　　B) 459　　　　C) 461　　　　D) 462

27. $\frac{1}{3} \times \frac{1}{4} \times \frac{1}{5} \times 6 \times 8 \times 10 =$
    A) 8　　　　B) 6　　　　C) 4　　　　D) 2

28. On the planet dARNOC, the unit of currency is the gELF. If one gELF is equal to 25 cents, how many gELFs are equal to 3 dollars?
    A) 4　　　　B) 8　　　　C) 12　　　　D) 16

29. $9 \times 5 \times 2 \times 5 \times 2 \times 5 \times 2 =$
    A) 9000　　　B) 8900　　　C) 8090　　　D) 900

Go on to the next page ▐▶ **E**

30. $100 + 200 + 300 + 400 =$ A) 10^2 B) 10^3 C) 10^4 D) 10^{10}	30.
31. $2\times3\times5\times11\times37$ has the same value as A) 111×110 B) 15×825 C) 75×164 D) 30×405	31.
32. Find the missing number: $33\frac{1}{3}\%$ of $45 = \underline{\ ?\ }\times90$. A) $\frac{1}{3}$ B) $\frac{1}{6}$ C) $\frac{1}{15}$ D) $66\frac{2}{3}$	32.
33. The reciprocal of the reciprocal of the reciprocal of the reciprocal of $\frac{3}{4}$ is A) 0 B) 1 C) $\frac{3}{4}$ D) $\frac{4}{3}$	33.
34. $(2\times\frac{1}{100}) + (3\times\frac{1}{1000}) + (7\times\frac{1}{10000}) =$ A) 2.37 B) 0.237 C) 0.0237 D) 0.00237	34.
35. Chris is 7 years older than Dale. Terry is 4 years younger than Dale. Chris is how many years older than Terry? A) 11 B) 7 C) 4 D) 3	35.
36. How much less is the area of a rectangular field 60 meters by 40 meters than that of a square field with the same perimeter? A) 10 sq. m B) 100 sq. m C) 1000 sq. m D) they're equal	36.
37. What fractional part of $1\frac{1}{2}$ hours is $\frac{1}{2}$ minute? A) $\frac{1}{3}$ B) $\frac{1}{20}$ C) $\frac{1}{60}$ D) $\frac{1}{180}$	37.
38. Mutt and Jeff receive the same amount of money. Mutt buys 2 pens and has 80¢ left. Jeff buys 4 of these pens and has 30¢ left. What amount of money did each receive? A) 40¢ B) $1.30 C) 25¢ D) $1.80	38.
39. Find the last digit of 1983^{1984}. A) 1 B) 2 C) 3 D) 9	39.
40. A clock is set correctly at 2 P.M. It loses 3 minutes every hour. What is the correct time when the clock reads 9 A.M. the next day? A) 8 A.M. B) 8:03 A.M. C) 9:57 A.M. D) 10 A.M.	40.

The end of the contest ✍ **E**

Solutions on Page 57 · Answers on Page 86

1984-85 Elementary Grades Contest

for students in grades 5 & 6

Instructions

- **Time** You will have only _30 minutes_ working time for this contest. You might be _unable_ to finish all 40 questions in the time allowed.

- **Scores** Please remember that _this is a contest, not a test_—and there is no "passing" or "failing" score. Few students score as high as 30 points (75% correct). Students with half that, 15 points, _deserve commendation!_

- **Format and Point Value** This is a multiple-choice contest. Every answer is an A, B, C, or D. For each question, write your answer in the _Answers_ column to the right of the question. A correct answer is worth 1 point. Unanswered questions get no credit.

1. Which is largest? A) $1985+1985$ B) 1985×1985 C) $1985\div1985$ D) $1985-1985$	1.
2. $1221 + 1221 + 1221 + 1221 =$ A) 1221 B) 2442 C) 4224 D) 4884	2.
3. If Steve goes to sleep at 10:30 P.M. and sleeps for 9 hours and 30 minutes, he will wake at A) 11 A.M. B) 10 A.M. C) 9 A.M. D) 8 A.M.	3.
4. If $200 - 100$ is divided by $100 - 50$, the result is A) 2 B) 1 C) 0.5 D) 0	4.
5. In which of the following does "5" represent 5000? A) 3456 B) 34567 C) 345678 D) 3456789	5.
6. 0 divided by 1 is equal to A) $1 + 0$ B) $1 - 0$ C) 1×0 D) $\frac{1}{0}$	6.
7. Which is the largest number? A) $\frac{11}{7}$ B) $\frac{17}{7}$ C) $\frac{15}{7}$ D) 2	7.
8. One million = A) 1000000 B) 100000 C) 10000 D) 1000	8.
9. Which of the following numbers is *not* the square of an integer? A) 100 B) 200 C) 400 D) 900	9.
10. $(1\times1985) + (2\times1985) + (3\times1985) + (4\times1985) =$ A) 10×1985 B) 12×1985 C) 24×1985 D) 25×1985	10.
11. How many prime numbers are factors of 30? A) 0 B) 1 C) 2 D) 3	11.
12. $\frac{1}{2} + \frac{2}{4} + \frac{3}{6} + \frac{4}{8} =$ A) $\frac{1}{2}$ B) $1\frac{7}{8}$ C) 2 D) $2\frac{1}{8}$	12.
13. When a certain number is divided by 8, the quotient is 4 and the remainder is 0. The number is A) 2 B) 12 C) 24 D) 32	13.
14. At 7 A.M., the temperature in Montreal was 5 degrees below zero. At 1 P.M., the temperature was 5 degrees above zero. From 7 A.M. to 1 P.M., how many degrees did the temperature rise? A) 0 B) 5 C) 10 D) 25	14.
15. All of the following have 3 as a factor *except* A) 27 B) 57 C) 77 D) 87	15.

Go on to the next page ⫸ **E**

16. $\frac{42}{16} =$ 16.

   A) $2\frac{3}{8}$ B) $2\frac{1}{2}$ C) $2\frac{3}{4}$ D) $2\frac{5}{8}$

17. The least common multiple of 22 and 33 is   17.

   A) 11   B) 44   C) 66   D) 132

18. The largest prime factor of $22 \times 33 \times 55$ is   18.

   A) 1   B) 11   C) 5   D) $11 \times 11 \times 11$

19. There are 20 books on a shelf. If 12 books are removed, what percent of the number of original books was removed?   19.

   A) 8%   B) 12%   C) 40%   D) 60%

20. The cost of 4 shirts and 6 ties is $84. If each tie costs $4, each shirt costs   20.

   A) $6   B) $10   C) $15   D) $60

21. In the number 300 300, how many times greater is the value of the left-most "3" than the value of the right-most "3"?   21.

   A) 300   B) 1 000   C) 3 000   D) 100 000

22. The larger acute angle of a right triangle could *never* equal   22.

   A) 40°   B) 50°   C) 88°   D) 89°

23. The largest factor of 1985 which is less than 1985 is   23.

   A) 5   B) 397   C) 401   D) 1984

24. At the rate of 40¢ for the first 10 words and 3¢ for each additional word, the cost of a 15-word telegram is   24.

   A) 45¢   B) 55¢   C) 85¢   D) $4.15

25. $3 \times 3 \times 3 \times 2 \times 2 =$ 25.

   A) $3^2 \times 2^3$ B) 9×4 C) $6^2 \times 3$ D) 27×8

26. If a cat catches 7 mice in 4 days, how many mice should it catch in 16 days?   26.

   A) $4 \times 4 \times 4$ B) 4×7 C) $7 + 7$ D) 7×7

27. Find the product of the prime factors of 70.   27.

   A) 10   B) 14   C) 35   D) 70

28. A car is driven at the rate of 30 km per hour. The distance the car covers in one minute is   28.

   A) 15 km   B) 2 km   C) $\frac{1}{2}$ km   D) 4 km

29. A clerk addressed 140 letter during the first hour of a certain day, 120 letters during the second hour, and 170 letters during the third hour. How many letters must he address during the fourth hour in order to average 150 letters per hour for the four-hour period?   29.

   A) 130   B) 150   C) 160   D) 170

Go on to the next page ⟱ **E**

30. Which of the following has the least value? A) 0.1 B) 0.1÷0.1 C) 0.1×0.1 D) 0.1+0.1	30.
31. Mary got 34 questions right on a test and received a grade of 85%. The number of questions on the test was A) 50 B) 40 C) 38 D) 29	31.
32. The sum of three different whole numbers is 99. The largest number in this sum is 34. The smallest number in this sum is A) 33 B) 32 C) 31 D) 1	32.
33. Twenty telephone poles are placed in a straight line. The distance between any two consecutive poles is 4 meters. What is the distance between the 1st and 10th pole? A) 36 m B) 40 m C) 44 m D) 80 m	33.
34. If ■ × ▲ = 72 and ■ − ▲ = 71, then ■ + ▲ = A) 17 B) 27 C) 18 D) 73	34.
35. Which is an odd number? A) 2^{99} B) 3^{100} C) $(3+3)^3$ D) $(2+2+2)^2$	35.
36. The two circles in the diagram have the same center. A radius of the larger circle is 5 and a radius of the smaller circle is 2. The area of the shaded region is A) 6π B) 9π C) 21π D) 29π	36.
37. How many of the integers from 2 to 999 are squares of whole numbers? A) 30 B) 31 C) 60 D) 499	37.
38. The lengths of two sides of a triangle are 7 cm and 12 cm. The perimeter of the triangle *cannot* equal A) 23 cm B) 26 cm C) 30 cm D) 37 cm	38.
39. Four children line up at the lunch counter. In how many different orders can they arrange themselves in line? A) 4 B) 12 C) 20 D) 24	39.
40. Superman flew from Metropolis to Gotham City at 300 km/hr. He flew back from Gotham City to Metropolis at 600 km/hr (traveling the same distance each way). His average speed for the round trip was A) 400 km/hr B) 450 km/hr C) 500 km/hr D) 550 km/hr	40.

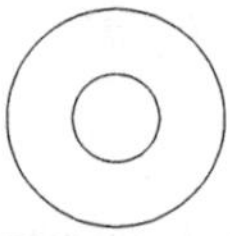

The end of the contest ✍ **E**

Solutions on Page 61 · Answers on Page 87

1985-86 Elementary Grades Contest

for students in grades 5 & 6

Instructions

- **Time** You will have only *30 minutes* working time for this contest. You might be *unable* to finish all 40 questions in the time allowed.

- **Scores** Please remember that *this is a contest, not a test*—and there is no "passing" or "failing" score. Few students score as high as 30 points (75% correct). Students with half that, 15 points, *deserve commendation!*

- **Format and Point Value** This is a multiple-choice contest. Every answer is an A, B, C, or D. For each question, write your answer in the *Answers* column to the right of the question. A correct answer is worth 1 point. Unanswered questions get no credit.

Answers

1. $(1986 - 1985) + (1984 - 1983) =$
   A) 0   B) 1   C) 2   D) 1982

   1.

2. Add the number of months in a year, the number of days in a week, and the number of minutes in an hour. The sum is
   A) 77   B) 79   C) 1760   D) 1960

   2.

3. $987 - 789 =$
   A) 202   B) 192   C) 198   D) 208

   3.

4. If John spends $5.42 on groceries and $7.29 on hardware, how much does John spend all together?
   A) $12.61   B) $12.71   C) $12.81   D) $12.91

   4.

5. $5 + 5 + 5 + 5 + 5 + 5 + 5 + 5 + 5 + 5 =$
   A) 5   B) 45   C) 50   D) 55

   5.

6. $(1 \times 9) + (2 \times 9) + (3 \times 9) + (4 \times 9) =$
   A) 89   B) 90   C) 99   D) 100

   6.

7. To increase 1986 by one thousand, add 1 to the digit
   A) 1   B) 9   C) 8   D) 6

   7.

8. $10 + (0 \times 10 \times 10 \times 10 \times 10) =$
   A) 0   B) 10   C) 50   D) 20 000

   8.

9. 230 hundreds $=$
   A) 23 000   B) 2 300   C) 230 000   D) 23 000 000

   9.

10. Of the following, which is the largest?
    A) 1983×1984 B) 1984×1985 C) 1985×1986 D) 1986×1987

    10.

11. $5 \times 5 \times 5 \times 5 =$
    A) 4^5 B) 5^4 C) 4×5 D) 5^5

    11.

12. The measure of one angle of an isosceles triangle is 20°. The measure of another angle of this triangle *could* be
    A) 20°   B) 40°   C) 60°   D) 180°

    12.

13. $\frac{1}{3} + \frac{1}{3} + \frac{1}{3} + \frac{1}{3} + \frac{1}{3} + \frac{1}{3} =$

    A) $\frac{6}{18}$ B) 1   C) 2   D) 3

    13.

14. The sum of 1 456 366 and 1 368 444 is
    A) 2 824 810   B) 2 824 812   C) 2 824 814   D) 2 824 816

    14.

15. The greatest common factor of 19 and 21 is
    A) 1   B) 2   C) 40   D) 19×21

    15.

16. Find the missing number: $4000 + 4000 = \underline{\ ?\ } + 8000.$
    A) 0   B) 1   C) 2000   D) 8000

    16.

Go on to the next page ⦀➡ **E**

17. A plane was supposed to land at 4:35 P.M. If the plane was 40 minutes late, it landed at
    A) 3:45 P.M.   B) 3:50 P.M.   C) 5:05 P.M.   D) 5:15 P.M.

17.

18. The smallest prime number between 20 and 30 is
    A) 21   B) 22   C) 23   D) 24

18.

19. A rectangle is divided into two squares, as seen in the diagram at the right. The area of each square is 16. The perimeter of the original rectangle is
    A) 16   B) 24   C) 28   D) 32

19.

20. Find the missing number: $4000 \times 2000 = 2000 \times \underline{\ ?\ }$
    A) 8000   B) 6000   C) 4000   D) 1000

20.

21. $9 \times 12345679 =$
    A) 111111119   B) 111111118   C) 111111113   D) 111111111

21.

22. On a 12-day trip, I spent $600. My average cost per day was
    A) $720   B) $612   C) $50   D) $20

22.

23. $2 \times 3 \times 4 \times 5 =$
    A) $6 \times 8 \times 10$ B) $4 \times 5 \times 6$ C) $4 \times 6 \times 10$ D) $3 \times 8 \times 10$

23.

24. Find the missing number: $1986 = 2 \times 3 \times \underline{\ ?\ }$
    A) 993   B) 662   C) 331   D) 111

24.

25. When a certain number is divided by 7, the quotient is 4 and the remainder is 3. This certain number is
    A) 7   B) 19   C) 25   D) 31

25.

26. Five children divided some cake equally. Two of the children together got what percent of the cake?
    A) 5%   B) 10%   C) 20%   D) 40%

26.

27. If I earn $1 every 20 minutes, how much do I earn in 24 hours?
    A) $3   B) $8   C) $24   D) $72

27.

28. $10\% + 20\% + 30\% + 40\% =$
    A) 1   B) 10   C) 100   D) 1000

28.

29. The cost of one liter of cola is half the cost of one liter of juice. If juice costs $2 per liter, the total cost of one liter of cola and one liter of juice is
    A) $2   B) $3   C) $4   D) $6

29.

30. If Al types 1 page each minute and Ann types 3 pages each minute, in how many minutes will Al be 100 pages behind Ann?
    A) 50   B) 100   C) 200   D) 300

30.

Go on to the next page IIII➡ **E**

31. If the first and last digits of each of the following numbers are interchanged, which will produce the *smallest* result? A) 8765　　　B) 7685　　　C) 6875　　　D) 8675	31.
32. In the diagram at the right, the illustrated arrow moves clockwise to the next number every hour. If the arrow points to the 6 right now, to which number will the arrow point in 24 hours? A) 2　　　B) 3　　　C) 6　　　D) 9	32.
33. After 5 tests, a student's average was 80. After taking an examination which counted as two test grades, his average dropped to 76. What was his grade on that examination? A) 52　　　B) 66　　　C) 72　　　D) 76	33.
34. Points A, B, and C lie on a straight line, and A is *not* between B and C. The distance from A to B is 15 cm. The distance from C to A is 8 cm. The distance from B to C is A) 23 cm　　　B) 20 cm　　　C) 10 cm　　　D) 7 cm	34.
35. The digits of 1986 are written in order from largest to smallest. Next, they're written in order from smallest to largest. The difference between the two 4-digit numbers thus formed is A) 8172　　　B) 8148　　　C) 7875　　　D) 4905	35.
36. A 12-hour clock loses 10 minutes each day. The clock will first return to the correct time in A) 36 days　　　B) 72 days　　　C) 120 days　　　D) 144 days	36.
37. A radius of circle I has the same length as a diameter of circle II. The ratio of circle I's area to circle II's area is A) 4 to 1　　　B) 2 to 1　　　C) 1 to 2　　　D) 1 to 4	37.
38. Bob earned \$33 in 6 days. At the same rate, Bob's total earnings should be \$88 in how many *more* days? A) 10　　　B) 14　　　C) 16　　　D) 22	38.
39. Which one of the following is most nearly equal to 6? A) $\dfrac{6.13 \times 5.89}{0.62}$　B) $\dfrac{61.3 \times 5.89}{0.62}$　C) $\dfrac{61.3 \times 5.89}{6.2}$　D) $\dfrac{0.613 \times 58.9}{6.2}$	39.
40. A positive number is called a *perfect square* whenever it is the square of a whole number. The first three perfect squares are 1, 4, and 9. The 100th perfect square is A) 100　　　B) 1000　　　C) 10 000　　　D) 100 000	40.

The end of the contest **E**

Solutions on Page 65 · Answers on Page 88

1991-92 Annual 4th Grade Contest

Spring, 1992

4

Instructions

- **Time** You will have only *30 minutes* working time for this contest. You might be *unable* to finish all 30 questions in the time allowed.

- **Scores** Please remember that *this is a contest, not a test*—and there is no "passing" or "failing" score. Few students score as high as 24 points (80% correct). Students with half that, 12 points, *deserve commendation!*

- **Format and Point Value** This is a multiple-choice contest. Each answer is an A, B, C, or D. Write each answer in the *Answer Column* to the right of each question. A correct answer is worth 1 point. Unanswered questions get no credit. You **may** use a calculator.

1991-92 4TH GRADE CONTEST

1. $0 + 0 + 0 + 0 + 0 + 0 + 0 + 0 + 0 + 0 =$

   A) 0 B) 1 C) 10 D) 11

2. Five years ago, I was 5 years old. Five years from now, I will be ? years old.

   A) 10 B) 15 C) 20 D) 25

3. $1 + 2 + 3 + 4 = 11 + 12 + 13 + 14 -$?

   A) 10 B) 15 C) 40 D) 50

4. Ten-thousand divided by two-thousand equals

   A) 5 B) 20 C) 5000 D) 8000

5. $2 + 2 + 2 + 2 =$

   A) 2 B) 2×2 C) $2 \times 2 \times 2$ D) $2 \times 2 \times 2 \times 2$

6. What is the remainder when 7778 is divided by 7?

   A) 0 B) 1 C) 2 D) 8

7. $30 \times 40 = 3 \times 4 \times$? .

   A) 0 B) 10 C) 100 D) 400

8. Which of the following sums is an odd number?

   A) 51 + 51 B) 36 + 63 C) 12 + 24 D) 49 + 51

9. If I have three dozen pens, then I have ? pens.

   A) 30 B) 36 C) 39 D) 42

10. $1 \times 9 \times 9 \times 2 =$

    A) 21 B) 162 C) 180 D) 1992

11. How many whole numbers are less than 1000?

    A) 997 B) 998 C) 999 D) 1000

12. If today is Monday, then 14 days from today will be

    A) Monday B) Tuesday C) Friday D) Sunday

Go on to the next page ▐▐▐➡ **4**

30

13. In the list of numbers 1, 2, 3, 4, 5, 6, 7, 8, 9, how many
    of the numbers in the list are exactly 2 more than some other
    number in the list?

    A) 2   B) 7   C) 9   D) 11

    13.

14. If bubble gum costs 5¢ per piece, the number of pieces that
    Ali can buy for $2.00 is

    A) 10   B) 20   C) 40   D) 195

    14.

15. What number must I multiply by 3 to get a product of 51?

    A) 153   B) 27   C) 17   D) 16

    15.

16. (1993 − 1992) ÷ (1992 − 1991) =

    A) 0   B) 1   C) 1991   D) 1992

    16.

17. John is 3 cm taller than Jim and 2 cm shorter than Jill. Jill is
    _?_ than Jim.

    A) 5 cm taller   B) 5 cm shorter
    C) 1 cm taller   D) 1 cm shorter

    17.

18. If Eric and Anna have been best friends for six and one-half
    years, they have been best friends for _?_ months.

    A) 65   B) 68   C) 72   D) 78

    18.

19. On a sheet of paper, a line is drawn
    through the center C of a square.
    How many times does this line inter-
    sect the sides of the square?

    ·C

    A) 0   B) 1   C) 2   D) 3

    19.

20. Of the following, which is the largest product?

    A) 47×53   B) 48×52   C) 49×51   D) 50×50

    20.

21. What is the time 16 minutes *before* 3:15 P.M.?

    A) 2:59 P.M.   B) 2:99 P.M.   C) 3:59 P.M.   D) 4:59 P.M.

    21.

22. 1234 + 5678 =

    A) 6666   B) 6789   C) 6912   D) 7032

    22.

Go on to the next page ⅢⅢ➡ **4**

23. I am going to retire when I am 65 years old. How old am I now if I am going to retire in 30 years? A) 20 B) 25 C) 30 D) 35	23.
24. If special stamps cost 17¢ each, how much does it cost to buy 8 of these special stamps? A) 25¢ B) 56¢ C) $1.26 D) $1.36	24.
25. $(50 - 40) + (40 - 30) + (30 - 20) + (20 - 10) =$ A) 50 B) 50 - 10 C) 50 + 10 D) 50 × 10	25.
26. What is the tens' digit of the *largest* 4-digit even number which uses each of the digits 5, 7, 8, and 9 exactly once? A) 9 B) 8 C) 7 D) 5	26.
27. When a certain number is divided by 3, the quotient is 240. When that same number is divided by 6, the quotient is A) 720 B) 480 C) 120 D) 80	27.
28. The Incredible Shrinking Boy becomes 4 cm shorter each year. If he is 2 m tall when he is 10 years old, how tall will he be when he is 25 years old? A) 140 cm B) 100 cm C) 60 cm D) 40 cm	28.
29. The product of 1000 whole numbers is 1000. What is the *largest* possible value the sum of these numbers can have? A) 1000 B) 1992 C) 1993 D) 1999	29.
30. Square *ABCD* is divided into four smaller squares, as shown in the diagram. The perimeter of each of the four smaller squares is 4. What is the perimeter of square *ABCD*? A) 8 B) 12 C) 16 D) 20	30.

The end of the contest ✍ **4**

Solutions on Page 69 · Answers on Page 89

1991-92 Annual 5th Grade Contest

Spring, 1992

5

Instructions

- **Time** You will have only *30 minutes* working time for this contest. You might be *unable* to finish all 30 questions in the time allowed.

- **Scores** Please remember that *this is a contest, not a test*—and there is no "passing" or "failing" score. Few students score as high as 24 points (80% correct). Students with half that, 12 points, *deserve commendation!*

- **Format and Point Value** This is a multiple-choice contest. Each answer is an A, B, C, or D. Write each answer in the *Answer Column* to the right of each question. A correct answer is worth 1 point. Unanswered questions get no credit. You **may** use a calculator.

1991-92 5TH GRADE CONTEST

		Answer Column
1. $(1992 + 1992) \times (1992 - 1992) =$ A) 0 B) 1 C) 1992 D) 3984		1.
2. Each of the following sums is less than 100 *except* A) $47 + 48$ B) $50 + 51$ C) $49 + 50$ D) $48 + 49$		2.
3. $703 + 307 =$ A) 110 B) 1010 C) 1100 D) 10010		3.
4. What is the product of the number of days in a week and the number of months in a year? A) 5 B) 19 C) 60 D) 84		4.
5. $(11 + 22 + 33) \div (1 + 2 + 3) =$ A) 10 B) 11 C) 30 D) 33		5.
6. Which of the following numbers has the *most* whole number factors? A) 4 B) 5 C) 8 D) 9		6.
7. Jack has seven dozen pencils and Jill has eight dozen pencils. How many more pencils does Jill have than Jack? A) 1 B) 12 C) 24 D) 96		7.
8. Each of the following sums is an even number *except* A) $977 + 111$ B) $282 + 828$ C) $189 + 891$ D) $949 + 494$		8.
9. The sum of 7 numbers is 567. Their average is A) 81 B) 88 C) 91 D) 98		9.
10. $1 + 2 + 3 + 4 + 5 = 11 + 12 + 13 + 14 + 15 - \underline{\ ?\ }$ A) 10 B) 16 C) 50 D) 100		10.
11. In what month does the 100th day of the year occur? A) March B) April C) May D) June		11.

Go on to the next page ▐▐▶ **5**

12. $1\times2\times3\times4\times5\times6 = 2\times12\times\underline{\ ?\ }$

    A) 18   B) 20   C) 24   D) 30

| 12. |

13. Which of the following numbers leaves a remainder of 1 when divided by 4?

    A) 37   B) 35   C) 31   D) 27

| 13. |

14. $1 + 22 + 333 + 4444 =$

    A) 4790   B) 4800   C) 5000   D) 5100

| 14. |

15. I own 1 white, 2 black, and 3 brown pigs. If all of these pigs could talk, how many of them could truthfully say "I am the same color as one or more of the other pigs."

    A) 3   B) 4   C) 5   D) 6

| 15. |

16. If Chip and Dale have been good friends for nine and one-half years, they have been good friends for $\underline{\ ?\ }$ months.

    A) 95   B) 104   C) 108   D) 114

| 16. |

17. The number 1992 has 4 digits. How many digits does the product $10\times10\times10\times10\times10\times10$ have, after it is simplified?

    A) 6   B) 7   C) 10   D) 1 000 000

| 17. |

18. Of the following, which *cannot* be the number of points in which a line can intersect (cross or touch) a circle?

    A) 3   B) 2   C) 1   D) 0

| 18. |

19. Ann *makes* 5 out of every 6 shots she tries when she plays basketball. Out of 30 shots Ann tries, she will *make* $\underline{\ ?\ }$ shots.

    A) 20   B) 24   C) 25   D) 29

| 19. |

20. Which of the following products is equal to 1 million?

    A) 10×10 B) 100×100 C) 1000×100 D) 1000×1000

| 20. |

21. Michael must be in school by 8 A.M. If Michael leaves his home at 7:21 A.M., he has $\underline{\ ?\ }$ minutes to get to school on time.

    A) 21   B) 29   C) 39   D) 79

| 21. |

Go on to the next page ⏵ **5**

22. Which of the following numbers is divisible by 15?		22.
A) 115 B) 215 C) 315 D) 415		
23. The sum of two consecutive whole numbers is 1993. What is the difference between these two numbers?		23.
A) 1 B) 2 C) 996 D) 1992		
24. If two different whole numbers are both less than 10, their product *could* equal		24.
A) 0 B) 1 C) 100 D) 101		
25. $(27 \times 31 \times 35 \times 39 \times 43) \div (43 \times 39 \times 35 \times 31) =$		25.
A) 1 B) 4 C) 5 D) 27		
26. The smallest odd number greater than 399 is divided by 10. The remainder of this division is		26.
A) 0 B) 1 C) 3 D) 9		
27. In rectangle *ABCD*, which of the following line segments is parallel to $\overline{BD}$?		27.
A) $\overline{AB}$ B) $\overline{CD}$ C) $\overline{BC}$ D) $\overline{AC}$		
28. Every prime between 30 and 100 has a ones' digit that is		28.
A) 1 B) 3 C) odd D) even		
29. If 5 gizmos = 3 gremlins, then 45 gremlins = _?_ gizmos.		29.
A) 27 B) 30 C) 47 D) 75		
30. A whole number is a *perfect square* if it can be expressed as the product of two equal whole numbers. For example, 9 is a perfect square since $9 = 3 \times 3$. How many perfect squares are greater than 0 and less than 1000?		30.
A) 30 B) 31 C) 32 D) 33		

The end of the contest ✍ **5**

Solutions on Page 73 · Answers on Page 90

1991-92 Annual 6th Grade Contest

March 10, 1992

6

Instructions

- **Time** You will have only *30 minutes* working time for this contest. You might be *unable* to finish all 40 questions in the time allowed.

- **Scores** Please remember that *this is a contest, not a test*—and there is no "passing" or "failing" score. Few students score as high as 30 points (75% correct). Students with half that, 15 points, *deserve commendation!*

- **Format and Point Value** This is a multiple-choice contest. Each answer is an A, B, C, or D. Write each answer in the *Answers* column to the right of each question. A correct answer is worth 1 point. Unanswered questions get no credit. You **may** use a calculator.

1. Add the number of days in January, March, April, May, June, July, August, September, October, November, and December. A) 334 B) 335 C) 336 D) 337	1.
2. When (1000 + 900 + 90 + 2) is divided by 5, the remainder is A) 1 B) 2 C) 3 D) 4	2.
3. (100 – 1) + (101 – 2) + (102 – 3) + (103 – 4) = 400 – _?_ . A) 0 B) 3 C) 4 D) 10	3.
4. If an even number is multiplied by 5, the ones' digit of the product is A) 0 B) 1 C) 2 D) 5	4.
5. $10^3 + (10^3 - 10^2) + (10^2 - 10) + (10 - 8) =$ A) 2008 B) 2002 C) 1998 D) 1992	5.
6. Find the missing number: 400 – 100 = _?_ – 50. A) 350 B) 300 C) 200 D) 150	6.
7. The sum of 5 nickels and 5 quarters has the same value as A) 3 dimes B) 8 dimes C) 10 dimes D) 15 dimes	7.
8. 7766 – 6677 = A) 1089 B) 1099 C) 1189 D) 1199	8.
9. Of the following, which has the *most* whole number divisors? A) 16 B) 34 C) 85 D) 121	9.
10. I multiplied my age by 4, added 20, divided by 2, and then subtracted twice my age. What number did I finally get? A) 0 B) 5 C) 10 D) 20	10.
11. In a leap year, the 70th day of the year will be March _?_ . A) 9th B) 10th C) 11th D) 12th	11.
12. Which of these numbers is *not* a factor of $(1 \times 2 \times 3 \times 4 \times 5 \times 6)$? A) 7 B) 8 C) 9 D) 10	12.
13. The average of eight 8's is A) 1 B) 8 C) 64 D) 88	13.
14. Ten-million divided by ten-thousand equals A) 10 B) 100 C) 1000 D) 10 000	14.
15. The time 475 minutes after 1:00 P.M. is A) 7:55 P.M. B) 8:45 P.M. C) 8:55 P.M. D) 9:55 P.M.	15.

Go on to the next page ⫸ **6**

16. $2^8 - 2^7 - 2^6 - 2^5 =$
    A) 2^5 B) 2^4 C) 2^3 D) 2^2

16.

17. Mark is twice his sister's age, and she is 6. If their mother's age is twice the sum of their ages, how old is their mother?
    A) 18   B) 24   C) 32   D) 36

17.

18. The sum of the measures of all the angles of a triangle is
    A) 180°   B) 120°   C) 90°   D) 60°

18.

19. Which of the following is *not* a factor of 7777?
    A) 7   B) 77   C) 777   D) 7777

19.

20. If 10% of 10% of a certain number is 2, this certain number is
    A) 20   B) 100   C) 120   D) 200

20.

21. If the space shuttle circles the earth once every half-hour, then in 24 hours the shuttle will circle the earth ? times.
    A) 48   B) 36   C) 24   D) 12

21.

22. When 57 999 is divided by 58, the quotient is ? and the remainder is 57.
    A) 1   B) 9   C) 99   D) 999

22.

23. The sum of the two prime numbers between 20 and 30 is
    A) 44   B) 50   C) 52   D) 54

23.

24. $\sqrt{1} + \sqrt{4} + \sqrt{9} + \sqrt{16} =$
    A) $\sqrt{10}$ B) $\sqrt{25}$ C) $\sqrt{30}$ D) $\sqrt{100}$

24.

25. The length of a side of a square is ? % of its perimeter.
    A) 4   B) 25   C) 40   D) 400

25.

26. A whole number is greater than 20 and less than 2000. What is the *smallest* possible value of the sum of all of its digits?
    A) 0   B) 1   C) 2   D) 3

26.

27. The greatest common factor of $4\times8\times12$ and $2\times4\times6$ is
    A) 4   B) 8   C) 12   D) 48

27.

28. The *prime* factorization of 72 is
    A) $2^2\times9$ B) $2^3\times 9$ C) $2^3\times3^2$ D) $2^2\times3^2$

28.

29. Which of the following symbols can replace the ♦ and convert the statement (77×888) ♦ (88×777) into a true statement?
    A) <   B) =   C) >   D) ≠

29.

30. Which of the following numbers *cannot* be expressed as the product of two consecutive whole numbers?
    A) 0   B) 2   C) 56   D) 63

30.

Go on to the next page ⬛➡ **6**

39

31. What is the fewest number of squares, each with a perimeter of 4, that would completely cover a square with a side of 4? A) 1 B) 4 C) 8 D) 16	31.
32. The sum of five different positive integers is 500. The largest possible value for one of these integers is A) 102 B) 490 C) 494 D) 499	32.
33. The average of six numbers is 12. Subtract 6 from one of these numbers. The six numbers would then have an average of A) 6 B) 10 C) 11 D) 12	33.
34. I write 1992 different whole numbers. The difference between the *number* of even numbers I wrote and the *number* of odd numbers I wrote can equal any of the following *except* A) 0 B) 700 C) 1111 D) 1992	34.
35. The length of each side of a hexagon is a whole number. The perimeter of this hexagon *cannot* equal A) 5 B) 1991 C) 1992 D) 1993	35.
36. The difference between two prime numbers can *never* equal A) 1 B) 2 C) 7 D) 8	36.
37. A circle and a square intersect so that two sides of the square are also radii of the circle. If a side of the square is 2, what is the area of the shaded region? A) $4\pi - 4$ B) $4 - \pi$ C) $2\pi - 4$ D) $\pi - 2$	37.
38. In a list of 200 numbers, each number after the first number is 4 more than the number that comes before it. What is the difference between the first and the last number on this list? A) 200 B) 796 C) 800 D) 804	38.
39. The sum of the squares of the first 20 positive integers is 2870. What is the sum of the squares of the first 19 positive integers? A) 2350 B) 2361 C) 2470 D) 2850	39.
40. My dog was 100 m from home, and my cat was 80 m from home. I called them, and they both ran directly home. If my dog ran twice as fast as my cat, how far from home was my cat when my dog reached home? A) 20 m B) 30 m C) 40 m D) 50 m	40.

The end of the contest **6**

Solutions on Page 77 · Answers on Page 91

Detailed Solutions

● ● ● ● ● ● ● ● ● ● ● ● ● ● ● ●

1979-80 through 1985-86

Solutions

1979-80 Elementary Grades Contest

for students in grades 5 & 6

E

Contest Information

- **Solutions** Turn the page for detailed contest solutions (written in the question boxes) and letter answers (written in the *Answers* column to the right of each question).

- **Scores** Please remember that *this is a contest, not a test*—and there is no "passing" or "failing" score. Few students score as high as 30 points (75% correct). Students with half that, 15 points, *deserve commendation!*

- **Answers & Rating Scale** Turn to page 82 for the letter answers to each question and the rating scale for this contest.

1. Chickens have $10 \times 2 = 20$ legs and cows have $10 \times 4 = 40$ legs.
   A) 20   B) 40   C) 60   D) 80

   1. C

2. $\dfrac{5075}{25} = 5075 \div 25 = 203$.

   A) 23   B) 203   C) 213   D) 230

   2. B

3. A diameter equals twice a radius, so the diameter is $2 \times 8 = 16$.
   A) 4 cm   B) 8 cm   C) 16 cm   D) 64 cm

   3. C

4. $2.7 - 1.8 = (2.7 - 1.7) - 0.1 = 1.0 - 0.1 = 0.9$.
   A) 4.5   B) 1.9   C) 1.1   D) 0.9

   4. D

5. There are 4 rows with 12 dots in each row. Therefore, the total number of dots in the drawing at the right is $4 \times 12 = 48$.
   A) 28   B) 32   C) 48   D) 60

   5. C

6. $42 \times 79 - 79 \times 42 = 42 \times 79 - 42 \times 79 = 0$.
   A) 0   B) 1659   C) 3318   D) 6636

   6. A

7. 1849 is between 1800 and 1900, but it is closer to 1800.
   A) 1800   B) 1850   C) 1900   D) 2000

   7. A

8. $\dfrac{2 \times 2 \times 2 \times 2}{2 + 2 + 2 + 2} = \dfrac{16}{8} = 16 \div 8 = 2$.
   A) 0   B) 1   C) 2   D) 4

   8. C

9. Since $12 = 6 \times 2$ and $18 = 6 \times 3$, their greatest common factor is 6.
   A) 6   B) 12   C) 18   D) 36

   9. A

10. $10-9 + 8-7 + 6-5 + 4-3 + 2-1 = 1 + 1 + 1 + 1 + 1 = 5$.
    A) 45   B) 5   C) 4   D) 1

    10. B

11. The number of quarters in 8 dollars is $4 \times 8 = 32$.
    A) 2   B) 4   C) 16   D) 32

    11. D

12. Chris spent $\$1.21 + \$2.57 + \$1.94 = \$5.72$. Chris should receive $\$10.00 - \$5.72 = \$4.28$ change.
    A) \$5.72   B) \$5.28   C) \$4.72   D) \$4.28

    12. D

13. $13 \times 1000 + 13 \times 100 + 13 \times 1 = 13000 + 1300 + 13 = 14313$.
    A) 1313   B) 14313   C) 14413   D) 131313

    13. B

14. The least multiple of 10 that is divisible by 4 is 20.
    A) 2   B) 14   C) 20   D) 40

    14. C

15. $12\frac{1}{2}\%$ of $80 = \frac{1}{8} \times 80 = 10$.
    A) 10   B) 12   C) 16   D) 100

    15. A

Go on to the next page ⏵ **E**

16. Mary has 41¢ in coins. Since no two coins have the same value, she has a penny, a nickel, a dime, and a quarter, 4 coins in all. A) 4 B) 5 C) 6 D) 7	16. A
17. $12 \times 57 + 12 \times 43 = 12 \times (57 + 43) = 12 \times 100 = 1200$. A) 2400 B) 1298 C) 1296 D) 1200	17. D
18. A man needs six pieces of wire, each 218 centimeters long. This is a total of 6×218 cm = 1308 cm = 13.08 m. Since wire is sold only by the meter, the man must buy 14 m. A) 13 B) 14 C) 18 D) 1308	18. B
19. $2.25 \times 0.80 = 9/4 \times 4/5 = 9/5$, so choice C is correct. A) $1\frac{1}{2}$ B) $1\frac{3}{4}$ C) $1\frac{4}{5}$ D) 2	19. C
20. Since $2 \times 2 \times 2 \times 2 \times 2 \times 2 \times 2 = 128$, the answer is 7. A) 51 B) 7 C) 6 D) 5	20. B
21. $5 \times 1000 + 7 \times 100 + 3 \times 1 = 5000 + 700 + 3 = 5703$. A) 573 B) 5073 C) 5703 D) 5730	21. C
22. 2:3 as $(5 \times 2):(5 \times 3) = 10:15$, so choice B is correct. A) 9 B) 10 C) 14 D) 16	22. B
23. The average is $(0.3 + 0.03 + 0.003) \div 3 = 0.333 \div 3 = 0.111$. A) 0.111 B) 0.333 C) 0.666 D) 0.999	23. A
24. Since $51 = 3 \times 17$, 51 is *not* a prime number. A) 41 B) 51 C) 61 D) 71	24. B
25. Difference between the numbers is 2, 4, 6, 8. Next one is $21+10$. A) 37 B) 35 C) 33 D) 31	25. D
26. The 2 circles can intersect in 2 points and the line can intersect each circle in 2 points for a total of 6 points of intersection. A) 2 B) 4 C) 6 D) 8	26. C
27. $\frac{44 \times 55}{?} = \frac{4 \times 11 \times 5 \times 11}{?} = \frac{4 \times 5 \times 121}{?}$; if ? = 121, $\frac{4 \times 5 \times 121}{?} = 4 \times 5$. A) 11 B) 22 C) 45 D) 121	27. D
28. $\frac{1}{2}$ hour = 30 minutes. Commercials were shown for $\frac{5}{30} = \frac{1}{6}$ of the $\frac{1}{2}$ hour. A) $\frac{1}{5}$ B) $\frac{1}{6}$ C) $\frac{1}{10}$ D) $\frac{1}{12}$	28. B
29. $15/46 < 15/45 = 1/3$, so choice B is less than one-third. A) $\frac{5}{14}$ B) $\frac{15}{46}$ C) $\frac{31}{90}$ D) $\frac{104}{309}$	29. B

Go on to the next page ▌▶ **E**

30.	If 1 DRAC = \$1.70, then 10 DRACS = \$17.00 and 20 DRACS = \$34.00. A) 2 DRACS B) 17 DRACS C) 20 DRACS D) 34 DRACS	30. C
31.	$6^2 + 8^2 = 36 + 64 = 100 = 10^2$. A) 7^2 B) 10^2 C) 14^2 D) 28^2	31. B
32.	The number of seconds in 3.5 hrs $= 3.5 \times 60 \times 60 = 12\,600$. A) 210 B) 3 600 C) 10 800 D) 12 600	32. D
33.	Had he not divided by 5, he would have had 25. Had he multiplied the 25 by 5, as he should have, he would have had 125. A) 1 B) 25 C) 50 D) 125	33. D
34.	With 18 people, each got 12 apples. With only 12 people, each person would have gotten 18 apples. A) 6 B) 9 C) 18 D) 36	34. C
35.	Since $7 - 2 = 5$ have *only* tape recorders, $15 - 2 = 13$ have *only* pocket calculators, and exactly 2 have both, $30 - (5 + 13 + 2) = 30 - 20 = 10$ students have neither. A) 10 B) 8 C) 6 D) 4	35. A
36.	$\dfrac{1}{2 + \dfrac{1}{2 + \dfrac{1}{2 + \dfrac{1}{2}}}} = \dfrac{1}{2 + \dfrac{1}{2 + \dfrac{1}{\frac{5}{2}}}} = \dfrac{1}{2 + \dfrac{1}{\frac{12}{5}}} = \dfrac{1}{\frac{12}{5}} = \dfrac{5}{12}$. A) $\frac{1}{3}$ B) $\frac{2}{5}$ C) $\frac{2}{9}$ D) $\frac{5}{12}$	36. D
37.	The width of the walk is 5 on all 4 sides of the lot. The walk and lot form a 40×50 rectangle with area 2000. The lot's area is $30 \times 40 = 1200$, so the walk's area is 800. A) 800 m^2 B) 700 m^2 C) 375 m^2 D) 350 m^2	37. A
38.	Break all 3 links from 1 of the chains. This costs 15¢. If the remaining pieces of chain are A, B, and C, use the broken links to connect A & B, B & C, and A & C. This costs 15¢ + 18¢ = 33¢. A) 22¢ B) 33¢ C) 44¢ D) 88¢	38. B
39.	The average must be *halfway* between the middle 2 numbers. A) $36\frac{1}{3}$ B) $44\frac{1}{6}$ C) $48\frac{1}{2}$ D) 54	39. C
40.	There are 6 1×1's, 7 1×2's, 2 1×3's, 2 2×2's, and 1 2×3, for a total of $6+7+2+2+1 = 18$ rectangles in the diagram. A) 7 B) 9 C) 16 D) 18	40. D

The end of the contest ✍ **E**

Solutions

1980-81 Elementary Grades Contest

for students in grades 5 & 6

E

Contest Information

- **Solutions** Turn the page for detailed contest solutions (written in the question boxes) and letter answers (written in the *Answers* column to the right of each question).

- **Scores** Please remember that *this is a contest, not a test*—and there is no "passing" or "failing" score. Few students score as high as 30 points (75% correct). Students with half that, 15 points, *deserve commendation!*

- **Answers & Rating Scale** Turn to page 83 for the letter answers to each question and the rating scale for this contest.

1. The largest whole number less than 1000 is 1000 – 1 = 999. A) 99 B) 990 C) 999 D) 999.9	1. C
2. 148 + 149 + 150 + 151 + 152 = 5×150 = 750. A) 740 B) 750 C) 760 D) 770	2. B
3. 9/3 = 9÷3 = 3, so choice C is correct. A) $\frac{3}{3}$ B) $\frac{6}{3}$ C) $\frac{9}{3}$ D) $\frac{12}{3}$	3. C
4. Any product which contains 0 as a factor has a value of 0. A) 0 B) 15 C) 120 D) 1200	4. A
5. A rectangle has a length of 8 cm and a width of 5 cm. Its perimeter is 2×(8 + 5) = 2×13 = 26. A) 13 cm B) 26 cm C) 40 cm D) 80 cm	5. B
6. Since the team won 4 games and lost 20, it played 4 + 20 = 24 games. The fraction of games it won is 4/24 = 1/6. A) $\frac{1}{5}$ B) $\frac{1}{4}$ C) $\frac{4}{5}$ D) $\frac{1}{6}$	6. D
7. Numerator and denominator are the same, so $\frac{3\times4\times5\times6\times7}{7\times6\times5\times4\times3}=1$. A) 0 B) 0.2520 C) 1 D) 2520	7. C
8. $\frac{0}{10}$ = 0÷10 = 0. A) 0.10 B) 1 C) 0.1 D) 0	8. D
9. 10×100×1000 = 1000×1000 = 1000000. A) 1000000 B) 11000000 C) 100000000 D) 111000000	9. A
10. $6\times\frac{1}{2}\times\frac{1}{3}=6\times\frac{1}{6}=\frac{6}{6}$. A) 6 + 6 B) 6 – 6 C) 6×6 D) $\frac{6}{6}$	10. D
11. The perimeter of an equilateral triangle is 24 cm. Since all 3 sides are equal, the length of one side is 24÷3 = 8. A) 8 cm B) 12 cm C) 16 cm D) 72 cm	11. A
12. $\frac{32}{48}=\frac{32\div8}{48\div8}=\frac{4}{6}=\frac{4\div2}{6\div2}=\frac{2}{3}$. A) $\frac{2}{3}$ B) $\frac{3}{4}$ C) $\frac{5}{6}$ D) $\frac{11}{12}$	12. A
13. 0.91 + 0.19 = 0.91 + 0.09 + 0.10 = 1.00 + 0.10 = 1.10 = 1.1. A) 1.9 B) 1.1 C) 1.01 D) 1	13. B
14. 2.2 = 2.200, 2.02 = 2.020, and 2.00 = 2.000; choice A is largest. A) 2.2 B) 2.02 C) 2.002 D) 2.00	14. A
15. 1000000÷100 = 10000 = 10 thousand. A) 1 million B) 1 thousand C) 10 thousand D) 100 thousand	15. C

Go on to the next page ⮕ **E**

16. $\frac{1}{10} + \frac{2}{10} + \frac{3}{10} + \frac{4}{10} = \frac{10}{10} = 1.$

     A) $\frac{1}{4}$ B) $\frac{1}{2}$ C) $\frac{9}{10}$ D) 1

16. D

17. $1000 \times 968 = (10 \times 100) \times 968 = 10 \times (100 \times 968) = 10 \times 96\,800.$

     A) 0.968   B) 9.68   C) 96\,800   D) 968\,000

17. C

18. $0.1+0.3+0.5+0.7+0.9 = (0.1+0.9) + (0.3+0.7) + 0.5 = 5 \times 0.5.$

     A) 6×0.6 B) 5×0.5 C) 4×0.4 D) 3×0.3

18. B

19. $33\frac{1}{3}\%$ of $90 = \frac{1}{3} \times 90 = \frac{90}{3} = 90 \div 3 = 30.$

     A) 18   B) 27   C) 30   D) 45

19. C

20. Since $12 \div \frac{3}{4} = 16$, the actual distance between the towns is $16 \times 10 = 160$ miles.

     A) 90 miles   B) 120 miles   C) 150 miles   D) 160 miles

20. D

21. Any number which leaves a remainder of 1 when divided by 5 ends in 1 or 6. Since $351 = 7 \times 50 + 1$, choice C is correct.

     A) 153   B) 315   C) 351   D) 531

21. C

22. The sum of the digits of 111\,111\,111 is 9, a multiple of 3.

     A) 11\,111   B) 1\,111\,111   C) 11\,111\,111   D) 111\,111\,111

22. D

23. Sue had an average of 84 after 2 tests, so the sum of her scores was $2 \times 84 = 168$. Her average for 3 tests is $(168 + 96) \div 3 = 88.$

     A) 88   B) 90   C) 91   D) 92

23. A

24. $\frac{20}{32} = \frac{20 \div 4}{32 \div 4} = \frac{5}{8} = \frac{5 \times 3}{8 \times 3} = \frac{15}{24}$, so the missing number is 15.

     A) 15   B) 16   C) 17   D) 18

24. A

25. For any whole number, the 8th digit from the right is in the ten millions' place. For 987\,654\,321\,000, this digit is a 5.

     A) 4   B) 5   C) 6   D) 7

25. B

26. The prime numbers between 20 and 30 are 23 and 29.

     A) 1   B) 2   C) 3   D) 4

26. B

27. $\frac{1}{4} + 0.75 = 0.25 + 0.75 = 1.$

     A) 0.775   B) 0.95   C) 0.975   D) 1

27. D

28. Instead of a full brick on one side, change it to 2 half-bricks. Since 2 half-bricks balance a half-brick and a 6 lb. weight, a half-brick must weigh 6 lbs. So a full brick weighs $2 \times 6 = 12$ lbs.

     A) 3 lbs.   B) 6 lbs.   C) 9 lbs.   D) 12 lbs.

28. D

29. $\frac{1}{2}\% = 0.5\% = 0.5 \times 0.01 = 0.005.$

     A) 0.5   B) 0.05   C) 0.005   D) 0.0005

29. C

Go on to the next page ▥➡ **E**

30. The desired numbers are 2, 12, 20, 21, 23, 24, 25, 26, 27, 28, 29, 32, 42, 52, 62, 72, 82, and 92. There are 18 such numbers.

    A) 9   B) 18   C) 19   D) 20

    30. B

31. The *smallest* whole number divisor of 2468 greater than 1 is 2; the *largest* such divisor less than 2468 is $2468 \div 2 = 1234$.

    A) 2467   B) 1234   C) 842   D) 617

    31. B

32. $1+1 = 2, 1+2 = 3, \ldots, 5+8 = 13, 8+13 = 21.$

    A) 21   B) 20   C) 19   D) 15

    32. A

33. $\frac{1}{3} = \frac{2}{6} > \frac{2}{7} > \frac{2}{8} = \frac{1}{4}$, so choice B is correct.

    A) $\frac{2}{5}$ B) $\frac{2}{7}$ C) $\frac{2}{9}$ D) $\frac{2}{11}$

    33. B

34. The Hulk is 4 cm shorter than Superman, so the Hulk is 2 m – 4 cm = 200 cm – 4 cm = 196 cm tall. Tarzan is 3 cm shorter, so Tarzan's height is 196 cm – 3 cm = 193 cm.

    A) 193 cm   B) 197 cm   C) 203 cm   D) 207 cm

    34. A

35. $\dfrac{1}{\frac{1}{2}} + \dfrac{1}{\frac{1}{3}} = 1 \div \frac{1}{2} + 1 \div \frac{1}{3} = 1 \times 2 + 1 \times 3 = 2 + 3 = 5.$

    A) $\frac{5}{6}$ B) $\frac{5}{3}$ C) $\frac{12}{5}$ D) 5

    35. D

36. Lengths of other horizontal and vertical segments = known ones. $P = 2 \times (19+4)$.

    A) 15 and 26   B) 37 and 44   C) 45 and 55   D) 100 and 200

    36. C

37. If 5% of the number is 16, the number is 320; 25% of 160 = 40.

    A) 2   B) 4   C) 40   D) 80

    37. C

38. The palindromes between 100 and 200 are 101, 111, 121, 131, 141, 151, 161, 171, 181, and 191. Similarly, there are 10 palindromes beginning and ending with 2, with 3, . . ., and with 9. The number of palindromes between 100 and 1000 is $9 \times 10 = 90$.

    A) 9   B) 81   C) 90   D) 99

    38. C

39. Any such number must be divisible by $2 \times 2 \times 2 = 8$.

    A) 166   B) 168   C) 170   D) 172

    39. B

40. The clock loses 1 minute every 6 hours. From 6 A.M. on Jan. 1 to 6 A.M. on Jan. 6, the clock loses $5 \times 4 = 20$ min. From 6 A.M. to 12 noon on Jan. 6, the clock loses an additional 1 minute, for a total loss of 21 min.; 21 min. before 12 noon is 11:39 A.M.

    A) 11:36 A.M.   B) 11:38 A.M.   C) 11:39 A.M.   D) 11:40 A.M.

    40. C

The end of the contest ✍ **E**

Solutions

1981-82 Elementary Grades Contest

for students in grades 5 & 6

E

Contest Information

- **Solutions** Turn the page for detailed contest solutions (written in the question boxes) and letter answers (written in the *Answers* column to the right of each question).

- **Scores** Please remember that *this is a contest, not a test*—and there is no "passing" or "failing" score. Few students score as high as 30 points (75% correct). Students with half that, 15 points, *deserve commendation!*

- **Answers & Rating Scale** Turn to page 84 for the letter answers to each question and the rating scale for this contest.

1. $9999 + 2 = 9999 + 1 + 1 = 10000 + 1 = 10001$ A) 10001 B) 10011 C) 10101 D) 11111	1. A
2. In a 400-page book, each chapter has approximately 20 pages. Since $400 \div 20 = 20$, the book has approximately 20 chapters. A) 20 B) 40 C) 80 D) 8000	2. A
3. $1982 - 1892 = 1982 - (1882 + 10) = 1982 - 1882 - 10 = 90.$ A) 190 B) 170 C) 90 D) 70	3. C
4. $\frac{1+2+3}{3+4+5} = \frac{6}{12} = \frac{1}{2}.$ A) $\frac{43}{50}$ B) $\frac{1}{2}$ C) $\frac{1}{8}$ D) $\frac{1}{3}$	4. B
5. One soft drink cost 60¢ and one hamburger costs 75¢. Ten soft drinks and four hamburgers cost $10 \times 60¢ + 4 \times 75¢ = \$6 + \$3$. A) \$9 B) \$10 C) \$11 D) \$12	5. A
6. $6 \div \frac{1}{2} = 6 \times \frac{2}{1} = 6 \times 2 = 12.$ A) $\frac{1}{12}$ B) $\frac{1}{3}$ C) 3 D) 12	6. D
7. $(29 + 30) + 31 = 29 + (30 + 31)$, so choice A is correct. A) $29 + (30 + 31)$ B) $29 \times (30 + 31)$ C) $(29 + 31) + (30 + 31)$ D) $(29 \times 31) + (30 \times 31)$	7. A
8. When 112 is divided by 12, quotient is 9 and remainder is 4. A) 1 B) 2 C) 3 D) 4	8. D
9. $\frac{2}{11} + \frac{1}{22} + \frac{0}{33} = \frac{8}{44} + \frac{2}{44} + \frac{0}{44} = \frac{10}{44}$, so choice D is correct. A) 0 B) 3 C) 6 D) 10	9. D
10. $(4 \times 1000) + (7 \times 100) + (9 \times 1) = 4000 + 700 + 9 = 4709.$ A) 4790 B) 4709 C) 4079 D) 479	10. B
11. The largest number that leaves a remainder of 10 when divided into 90 must be $90 - 10 = 80$. A) 20 B) 40 C) 80 D) 100	11. C
12. $888888 \div 88 = (880000 + 8800 + 88) \div 88 = 10000 + 100 + 1 = 10101.$ A) 11111 B) 10101 C) 10001 D) 111	12. B
13. Since 7 and 9 are odd integers differing by 2, their GCF is 1. A) 1 B) 7 C) 9 D) 63	13. A
14. $(7 \times 87) + (3 \times 87) = (7 + 3) \times 87 = 10 \times 87 = 870.$ A) 860 B) 870 C) 880 D) 890	14. B
15. Area of a square each of whose sides is 3 cm long is $3 \times 3 = 9$. A) 6 sq. cm B) 9 sq. cm C) 12 sq. cm D) 81 sq. cm	15. B

Go on to the next page ▮▮▮➡ **E**

16. $\frac{19}{3} = 19 \div 3 = 6\frac{1}{3}$, so choice C is correct. A) $4\frac{1}{3}$ B) $5\frac{1}{3}$ C) $6\frac{1}{3}$ D) 16	16. C
17. Each number is less than 1, but choice B is closest to 1. A) $\frac{1}{1981}$ B) $\frac{1982}{1983}$ C) $\frac{1981}{1982}$ D) $\frac{1981}{1984}$	17. B
18. He walked (4 + 2) km north and (5 + 3) km south. In all, he walked 6 km north and 8 km south; he is 2 km south from start. A) 14 km north B) 14 km south C) 2 km north D) 2 km south	18. D
19. 1 hour = 60 minutes = (60×60) seconds = 3600 seconds. A) 60 B) 360 C) 3 600 D) 216 000	19. C
20. $\frac{1}{2} \times \frac{2}{3} \times \frac{3}{4} \times \frac{4}{5} \times \frac{5}{6} \times \frac{6}{7} \times \frac{7}{8} \times \frac{8}{9} = \frac{1}{1} \times \frac{1}{9} = \frac{1}{9}$. A) $\frac{1}{9}$ B) $\frac{3}{8}$ C) $\frac{856}{1279}$ D) $\frac{12345678}{23456789}$	20. A
21. Since 24÷8 = 3, the length of another side of the rectangle is 3 cm. The perimeter of the rectangle is 2×(3 cm + 8 cm) = 22 cm. A) 3 cm B) 11 cm C) 22 cm D) 24 cm	21. C
22. 0.1 – 0.01 = 0.10 – 0.01 = 0.09. A) 0 B) 0.09 C) 0.11 D) 0.99	22. B
23. Since $\frac{2}{3} = \frac{2 \times 2}{3 \times 2} = \frac{4}{6}$, the correct answer is choice A. A) multiplied by 2 B) increased by 2 C) decreased by 2 D) squared	23. A
24. 20% of 20 = 1/5×20 = 4. A) $\frac{1}{4}$ B) $\frac{1}{5}$ C) 0.4 D) 4	24. D
25. A right triangle has a 90° and two acute angles. The sum of the measures of the two smallest (acute) angles is 180° – 90° = 90°. A) 45° B) 90° C) 180° D) 360°	25. B
26. $3\frac{4}{25} = 3\frac{16}{100} = 3.16$. A) 3.8 B) 3.4 C) 3.16 D) 3.04	26. C
27. Since a quarter equals 5 nickels, the number of nickels in $1 is the same as the number of quarters in 5×$1 = $5. A) $4 B) $5 C) $20 D) $100	27. B
28. One million = 1000000 = 1000×1000 = one thousand thousands. A) one hundred thousands B) ten thousands C) one hundred hundreds D) one thousand thousands	28. D
29. Since 3 + 3 = 3×2, choice B is correct. A) 2 B) 3 C) 5 D) 6	29. B

Go on to the next page ⫸ **E**

30.	The length of one side of a regular hexagon is 30 cm. The perimeter of the hexagon is 6×30 cm $= 180$ cm. A) 5 cm B) 6 cm C) 150 cm D) 180 cm	30. D
31.	$2+2+3+2+2+3 = 14$; it's not a multiple of 3, so B is correct. A) 123123 B) 223223 C) 423423 D) 723723	31. B
32.	$4 \times 4 \times 4 \times 4 \times 4 = 2 \times 2 \times 2 \times 2 \times 2 \times 2 \times 2 \times 2 \times 2 \times 2 = 2^{10}$. A) 5^4 B) 4×5 C) 4^4 D) 2^{10}	32. D
33.	The place-value of the left-most "1" is 100000 and the place-value of the right-most "1" 10000. The difference is 90000. A) 10 B) 100 C) 90000 D) 100000	33. C
34.	From 1982 to 2000 is 19 tickets, from 2001 to 2100 is 100 tickets, and from 2101 to 2132 is 32 tickets. In all, Dale sold (19 + 100 + 32) tickets = 151 tickets. A) 149 B) 150 C) 151 D) 250	34. C
35.	The average of three numbers is 20. Suppose that the first number is increased by 1, the second number is increased by 2, and the third number is increased by 3. The average of the three numbers has been increased by $(1 + 2 + 3) \div 3 = 6 \div 3 = 2$. A) 1 B) 2 C) 3 D) 6	35. B
36.	After a girl spends $\frac{1}{3}$ of her money, she has $\frac{2}{3}$ left. If she loses $\frac{1}{2}$ of this, she has $\frac{1}{3}$ left. Since $\frac{1}{3} = \$10$, $\frac{3}{3} = 3 \times \$10 = \$30$. A) \$30 B) \$45 C) \$50 D) \$60	36. A
37.	Let's use the example of 25 students in the class. Then, there would be 10 boys and 15 girls, since $10 \div 15 = 2{:}3$. There are 10 boys out of 25 students, so 10/25 of them, 40%, are boys. A) 20% B) 40% C) 60% D) $66\frac{2}{3}\%$	37. B
38.	If 60 m of uniform wire weighs 80 grams, 1 m weighs $(80 \div 60)$ grams and 141 m weighs $(141 \times 80) \div 60$ grams = 188 grams. A) 160 grams B) 162 grams C) 165 grams D) 188 grams	38. D
39.	It's just like a magic square! The sum of all 12 numbers is 78. Hence, the answer is $78 \div 3 = 26$. A) 18 B) 21 C) 26 D) 32	39. C
40.	Flipping *doesn't* work, since a flip of 1981 would give a backwards 6, not a 6. Turning the paper upside down doesn't work, since 1981 would turn into 1861. Separately turn each digit 180°. The 8 years are 1986, 1988, 1989, 1990, 1991, 1996, 1998, & 1999. A) 6 B) 7 C) 8 D) 9	40. C

The end of the contest 👈 **E**

Solutions

1982-83 Elementary Grades Contest

for students in grades 5 & 6

E

Contest Information

- **Solutions** Turn the page for detailed contest solutions (written in the question boxes) and letter answers (written in the *Answers* column to the right of each question).

- **Scores** Please remember that *this is a contest, not a test*—and there is no "passing" or "failing" score. Few students score as high as 30 points (75% correct). Students with half that, 15 points, *deserve commendation!*

- **Answers & Rating Scale** Turn to page 85 for the letter answers to each question and the rating scale for this contest.

1. $(1+9+8+3) - (3+8+9+1) = (1+9+8+3) - (1+9+8+3) = 0.$ A) 0 B) 1 C) 2 D) 3	1. A
2. $98 + 98 + 98 + 98 + 98 + 98 + 98 + 98 + 98 + 98 = 10 \times 98 = 980.$ A) 962 B) 970 C) 972 D) 980	2. D
3. Since $(4 \times 4)/4 = 16/4 = 4$, choice B is correct. A) $\frac{44}{4}$ B) $\frac{4 \times 4}{4}$ C) $44 - 4$ D) $(4 \times 4) - 4$	3. B
4. $2 \times 3 \times 4 \times 5 = (2 \times 3) \times (4 \times 5) = 6 \times 20.$ A) 6×20 B) $2 \times 10 \times 12$ C) $6 \times 8 \times 10$ D) $6 \times 4 \times 6 \times 5$	4. A
5. $(27 + 29) + (73 + 71) = (27 + 73) + (29 + 71) = 100 + 100 = 200.$ A) 100 B) 180 C) 200 D) 220	5. C
6. There are 4 prime numbers between 0 and 10: 2, 3, 5, and 7. A) 3 B) 4 C) 5 D) 6	6. B
7. $\frac{1}{9} + \frac{3}{9} + \frac{5}{9} = \frac{9}{9} = 1.$ A) $\frac{1}{3}$ B) 1 C) $\frac{10}{9}$ D) $\frac{5}{243}$	7. B
8. From 9:00 A.M. one day to 9:00 A.M. the next is 24 hrs. From 9:00 A.M. to 1:00 P.M. is 4 hrs; total is $24 + 4 = 28$ hrs. A) 4 hours B) 16 hours C) 24 hours D) 28 hours	8. D
9. $2 \times \frac{1}{2} \times 2 \times \frac{1}{2} \times 2 = (2 \times \frac{1}{2}) \times (2 \times \frac{1}{2}) \times 2 = 1 \times 1 \times 2 = 2.$ A) 4 B) 2 C) 1 D) $\frac{1}{2}$	9. B
10. The average of 74, 76, and 81 is $(74 + 76 + 81) \div 3 = 77.$ A) 75 B) 76 C) 77 D) 78	10. C
11. Only choice D does not have line segments as sides. A) triangle B) rhombus C) square D) circle	11. D
12. Chris walked $(2 + 4 + 6)$ km east and $(3 + 2)$ km west. In all, Chris walked 12 km east and 5 km west. Chris is now $12 - 5 = 7$ kilometers away from school. A) 0 B) 7 C) 10 D) 17	12. B
13. The sum of the digits of 1983 is 21, a multiple of 3. A) 1981 B) 1982 C) 1983 D) 1984	13. C
14. $0.2 \times 0.5 = 1/5 \times 1/2 = 1/10 = 0.1.$ A) 1 B) 0.1 C) 0.01 D) 0.001	14. B
15. $5 + (10 \times 8) + (100 \times 9) + (1000 \times 2) = 5 + 80 + 900 + 2000 = 2985.$ A) 5892 B) 5111 C) 1115 D) 2985	15. D
16. Since $100 \div 6 = 16\frac{2}{3}$, choice B is correct. A) 15 B) 16 C) 17 D) 95	16. B

Go on to the next page ▐▐▶ **E**

17. 4 cm = (4÷100) m = 0.04 m. A) 400 m B) 40 m C) 0.4 m D) 0.04 m	17. D
18. The sum of the digits of 7472 is 7 + 4 + 7 + 2 or 20. The sum of the digits of 99 999 999 999 999 999 999 is 20×9 = 180. A) 20 B) 171 C) 180 D) 999	18. C
19. 0.1919+0.9191 = (0.19+0.91)+(0.0019+0.0091) = 1.10+.011 = 1.111. A) 1 B) 1.1 C) 1.11 D) 1.111	19. D
20. The perimeter of a rectangle is 48 cm. Half the perimeter = 24 = length + width. Since the length is 16, the width is 24 − 16 = 8. A) 3 cm B) 8 cm C) 16 cm D) 32 cm	20. B
21. 16161616÷8 = (16000000+160000+1600+16)÷8 = 2020202 A) 2222 B) 20222 C) 202022 D) 2020202	21. D
22. The number of boys that leave the room must equal the number of boys that remain. Since 5 boys leave, there are 5 boys still in the room for a total of 10 boys. A) 5 B) 10 C) 15 D) 20	22. B
23. $12×(\frac{1}{2}+\frac{1}{3}+\frac{1}{4}) = 12×\frac{1}{2}+12×\frac{1}{3}+12×\frac{1}{4} = 6+4+3 = 13.$ A) 72 B) 13 C) $\frac{4}{3}$ D) $\frac{1}{2}$	23. B
24. $12×(\frac{1}{2}×\frac{1}{3}×\frac{1}{4}) = (12×\frac{1}{2})×\frac{1}{3}×\frac{1}{4} = 6×\frac{1}{3}×\frac{1}{4} = 2×\frac{1}{4} = \frac{2}{4} = \frac{1}{2}.$ A) 72 B) 13 C) $\frac{4}{3}$ D) $\frac{1}{2}$	24. D
25. The side of each small square is 3, so each side of the largest square is 3×3 = 9. The perimeter of the largest square is 4×9 = 36. A) 12 B) 36 C) 81 D) 108	25. B
26. 50% of 50% of 50% of 100% is 1/2×1/2×1/2×100% = 12.5%. A) 125% B) 12.5% C) 1.25% D) 0.125%	26. B
27. A Strangus year has 15×7×5 = 525 days. A) 27 days B) 425 days C) 525 days D) 625 days	27. C
28. It take this genius 31 000÷100 = 310 seconds = 5 mins. 10 secs. to read 31 000 words backwards. A) 5 minutes, 10 seconds B) 5 minutes, 30 seconds C) 5 minutes, 20 seconds D) 5 minutes, 40 seconds	28. A
29. (6 days 7 hrs. 35 mins.)−(3 days 9 hrs. 50 mins.) = (5 days 30 hrs. 95 mins.)−(3 days 9 hrs. 50 mins.) = 2 days 21 hrs. 45 mins. A) 2 days 22 hours 45 minutes B) 2 days 21 hours 45 minutes C) 2 days 7 hours 15 minutes D) 2 days 2 hours 15 minutes	29. B

Go on to the next page ⏵ **E**

30. The longest line segment that can be drawn between two points on a circle is a diameter. Since a radius of this circle is 20 cm, a diameter is 40 cm. The line segment *cannot* be 50 cm. A) 50 cm B) 40 cm C) 2 cm D) 1 cm	30. A
31. Count the man, his 10 sons, and their 100 sons. All together, there are $1 + 10 + 100 = 111$ people. A) 21 B) 100 C) 101 D) 111	31. D
32. For \$1, you could buy either 5 apples (at 20¢ each) or 4 oranges (at 25¢ each). The desired ratio is $20{:}25 = 4{:}5$. A) 5:9 B) 4:9 C) 5:4 D) 4:5	32. D
33. $\frac{1}{2} = \frac{1 \times 8.5}{2 \times 8.5} = \frac{8.5}{17}$, so choice A is correct. A) 8.5 B) 1.7 C) 17 D) 34	33. A
34. Since there are already 4 arrows pointing down, turn the 6 other arrows so that all the arrows point down. A) 4 B) 5 C) 6 D) 11	34. C
35. The *Blackjack* years between 1900 and 2000 are 1929, 1938, 1947, 1956, 1965, 1974, 1983, and 1992. There are 8 *Blackjack* years between 1900 and 2000. A) 10 B) 9 C) 8 D) 7	35. C
36. Choice A is 1/100 more than 1/2; the others are closer to 1/2. A) $\frac{51}{100}$ B) $\frac{152}{300}$ C) $\frac{52}{103}$ D) $\frac{50}{99}$	36. A
37. Joan paid $\$10 + \$30 = \$40$ for the painting; she sold it for $\$20 + \$40 = \$60$. Joan made $\$60 - \$40 = \$20$. A) broke even B) made \$20 C) lost \$10 D) lost \$20	37. B
38. If a chicken lays 1 egg in 1 minute, each chicken will lay 1 egg each minute, so 3 chickens will lay a total of 3 eggs in 1 min. A) $\frac{1}{3}$ B) 1 C) 3 D) 9	38. B
39. $\frac{3}{5}$ exceeds $\frac{2}{5}$ by $\frac{1}{5}$, and $\frac{1}{5}$ is 25% of $\frac{4}{5}$; 25% $= \frac{1}{4}$, so B is correct. A) $\frac{1}{5}$ B) $\frac{1}{4}$ C) $\frac{2}{5}$ D) $\frac{3}{5}$	39. B
40. Each number on the right side is 1 less than the corresponding number on the left. There are $1984 \div 2 = 992$ numbers on the left. A) 992 B) 1984 C) 1985 D) 3968	40. A

The end of the contest ✍ **E**

Solutions

1983-84 Elementary Grades Contest

for students in grades 5 & 6

E

Contest Information

- **Solutions** Turn the page for detailed contest solutions (written in the question boxes) and letter answers (written in the *Answers* column to the right of each question).

- **Scores** Please remember that *this is a contest, not a test*—and there is no "passing" or "failing" score. Few students score as high as 30 points (75% correct). Students with half that, 15 points, *deserve commendation!*

- **Answers & Rating Scale** Turn to page 86 for the letter answers to each question and the rating scale for this contest.

		Answers
1.	1984 + 1 = 1985, so choice D is correct. A) 1984 + 0 B) 1984×1 C) 1984÷1 D) 1984 + 1	1. D
2.	$\frac{13}{13} + \frac{15}{15} + \frac{17}{17} + \frac{19}{19} = 1 + 1 + 1 + 1 = 4.$ A) 1 B) $\frac{66}{19}$ C) 2 D) 4	2. D
3.	The sum is always odd. For example, 15 + 10 = 25. A) an odd number B) an even number C) a prime number D) a multiple of 3	3. A
4.	111 111 111 divided by 9 equals 12 345 679, so choice B is correct. A) 12 345 678 B) 12 345 679 C) 12 345 789 D) 12 345 799	4. B
5.	1 000 000 – 101 = 1 000 000 – 100 – 1 = 999 900 – 1 = 999 899. A) 999 999 B) 999 989 C) 999 899 D) 999 889	5. C
6.	Each number is less than 1, but choice B is closest to 1. A) $\frac{4}{5}$ B) $\frac{5}{6}$ C) $\frac{2}{3}$ D) $\frac{3}{4}$	6. B
7.	32 123 + 12 321 = 44 444, so choice A is correct. A) 44 444 B) 54 444 C) 55 555 D) 45 454	7. A
8.	Choose the number where 2 is in the third place from the right. A) 1423 B) 2134 C) 1234 D) 4132	8. C
9.	9998 + 9999 + 10000 + 10001 + 10002 = 5×10000 = 50000. A) 49998 B) 49999 C) 50000 D) 50001	9. C
10.	$\frac{7}{6} + \frac{8}{6} + \frac{9}{6} = \frac{7+8+9}{6} = \frac{24}{6} = 24÷6 = 4.$ A) 5 B) 4 C) 3 D) 2	10. B
11.	(876×543) – (543×876) = (876×543) – (876×543) = 0. A) 0 B) 1 C) 237 834 D) 475 668	11. A
12.	The sum of the measures of all three angles of *any* triangle is 180°. A) 90° B) 150° C) 180° D) 360°	12. C
13.	0.33 = 33÷100 = 33/100, so choice B is correct. A) $\frac{3}{10}$ B) $\frac{33}{100}$ C) $\frac{1}{3}$ D) $\frac{3}{8}$	13. B
14.	Since three-fifths of the students are girls, two-fifths are boys. The number of boys in the class is 2/5×30 = 12. A) 6 B) 12 C) 18 D) 24	14. B
15.	$20÷\frac{1}{2} = 20×\frac{2}{1} = 20×2 = 40.$ A) 40 B) 10 C) 5 D) 2	15. A

Go on to the next page ▶ **E**

16. The whole numbers which leave no remainder when divided into 60 are the *factors* of 60: 1, 2, 3, 4, 5, 6, 10, 12, 15, 20, 30, & 60.
A) 10 B) 12 C) 15 D) 30

16.
B

17. $\frac{1+2+3+4+5}{1\times2\times3\times4\times5} = \frac{15}{120} = \frac{15\div5}{120\div5} = \frac{3}{24} = \frac{1}{8}.$
A) 0 B) $\frac{1}{8}$ C) 1 D) 8

17.
B

18. $1984 = 2\times2\times2\times2\times2\times2\times31$, so 31 is its largest prime factor.
A) 23 B) 29 C) 31 D) 64

18.
C

19. The number of minutes in 4 hours $= 4\times60 = 4\times6\times10 = 24\times10 =$ the number of hours in 10 days.
A) 4 days B) 6 days C) 10 days D) 60 days

19.
C

20. Since $23\times\underline{?} = 1081$, $\underline{?} = 1081\div23 = 47$.
A) 43 B) 47 C) 57 D) 1058

20.
B

21. Multiplying a number by $\frac{1}{100}$, is the same as dividing by 100. When dividing by 100, move the decimal point 2 places left.
A) two places to the left B) one place to the left
C) two places to the right D) one place to the right

21.
A

22. The smallest multiple of 30 which is divisible by 12 & 18 is 180.
A) 6 B) 60 C) 180 D) 540

22.
C

23. $1\frac{2}{3} + 2\frac{1}{2} = 1\frac{4}{6} + 2\frac{3}{6} = 3\frac{7}{6} = 4\frac{1}{6}.$
A) $3\frac{3}{5}$ B) $3\frac{5}{6}$ C) $4\frac{1}{6}$ D) $4\frac{1}{3}$

23.
C

24. If a diameter of a circle is 20, then a radius is $\frac{1}{2}\times20 = 10$.
A) 40 B) 40π C) 10 D) 10π

24.
C

25. $\frac{6666}{33} = 6666\div33 = 6600\div33 + 66\div33 = 200 + 2 = 202.$
A) 2222 B) 2020 C) 222 D) 202

25.
D

26. The average of 473 and 449 is 461, so choice D is correct.
A) 455 B) 459 C) 461 D) 462

26.
D

27. $\frac{1}{3}\times\frac{1}{4}\times\frac{1}{5}\times6\times8\times10 = \frac{1}{3}\times6\times\frac{1}{4}\times8\times\frac{1}{5}\times10 = 2\times2\times2 = 8.$
A) 8 B) 6 C) 4 D) 2

27.
A

28. Since 1 gELF = 25¢, 4 gELFs = 4×25¢ = $1. Since 4 gELFs = $1, 3×4 gELFs = $3\times$$1 or 12 gELFs = $3.
A) 4 B) 8 C) 12 D) 16

28.
C

29. $9\times5\times2\times5\times2\times5\times2 = 9\times10\times10\times10 = 9\times1000 = 9000.$
A) 9000 B) 8900 C) 8090 D) 900

29.
A

Go on to the next page ▌▌▌➡ **E**

30.	$100+200+300+400 = (1+2+3+4)\times100 = 10\times100 = 1000 = 10^3$. A) 10^2 B) 10^3 C) 10^4 D) 10^{10}	30. B
31.	$2\times3\times5\times11\times37 = (3\times37)\times(2\times5\times11) = 111\times110$. A) 111×110 B) 15×825 C) 75×164 D) 30×405	31. A
32.	$33\frac{1}{3}\%\times45 = \frac{1}{3}\times45 = (\frac{1}{2}\times2)\times\frac{1}{3}\times45 = (\frac{1}{2}\times\frac{1}{3})\times(2\times45) = 1/6\times90$. A) $\frac{1}{3}$ B) $\frac{1}{6}$ C) $\frac{1}{15}$ D) $66\frac{2}{3}$	32. B
33.	Each pair of reciprocals leaves $\frac{3}{4}$. Since there are two pairs of reciprocals, choice C is correct. A) 0 B) 1 C) $\frac{3}{4}$ D) $\frac{4}{3}$	33. C
34.	$(2\times\frac{1}{100}) + (3\times\frac{1}{1000}) + (7\times\frac{1}{10000}) = 0.02 + 0.003 + 0.0007 = 0.0237$. A) 2.37 B) 0.237 C) 0.0237 D) 0.00237	34. C
35.	Since Chris is 7 years older than Dale and Terry is 4 years younger than Dale, Chris is $7 + 4 = 11$ years older than Terry. A) 11 B) 7 C) 4 D) 3	35. A
36.	Perimeter of field is $2\times(60+40) = 200$ and its area is 2400. A side of the square is $200\div4 = 50$; its area is 2500. They differ by 100. A) 10 sq. m B) 100 sq. m C) 1000 sq. m D) they're equal	36. B
37.	$1\frac{1}{2}$ hrs. $= 90$ minutes; $\frac{1}{2}:90 = 2\times\frac{1}{2}:2\times90 = 1:180$. A) $\frac{1}{3}$ B) $\frac{1}{20}$ C) $\frac{1}{60}$ D) $\frac{1}{180}$	37. D
38.	Since 2 additional pens left Jeff with 50¢ less than Mutt, each pen must cost 50¢$\div2 = 25$¢. Since Mutt bought 2 pens and has 80¢ left, he began with 2×25¢ $+ 80$¢ $= \$1.30$. A) 40¢ B) \$1.30 C) 25¢ D) \$1.80	38. B
39.	Pattern of ones' digits is 3, 9, 7, 1, 3, 9, 7, 1, ... 1984th is a 1. A) 1 B) 2 C) 3 D) 9	39. A
40.	For each real hour, the clock shows only 57 mins. The pattern of corresponding real and clock times is **real:** 2 PM 3 PM 4 PM . . . 9 AM 10 AM; **clock:** 2 PM 2:57 3:54 . . . 7:06 8:03 9 AM. A) 8 A.M. B) 8:03 A.M. C) 9:57 A.M. D) 10 A.M.	40. D

The end of the contest ✍ **E**

60

Solutions

1984-85 Elementary Grades Contest

for students in grades 5 & 6

E

Contest Information

- **Solutions** Turn the page for detailed contest solutions (written in the question boxes) and letter answers (written in the *Answers* column to the right of each question).

- **Scores** Please remember that *this is a contest, not a test*—and there is no "passing" or "failing" score. Few students score as high as 30 points (75% correct). Students with half that, 15 points, *deserve commendation!*

- **Answers & Rating Scale** Turn to page 87 for the letter answers to each question and the rating scale for this contest.

1. $1985 \times 1985 > 1000 \times 1000 = 1000000$, so choice B is largest. A) $1985+1985$ B) 1985×1985 C) $1985 \div 1985$ D) $1985-1985$	1. B
2. $1221 + 1221 + 1221 + 1221 = 4 \times 1221 = 4884$. A) 1221 B) 2442 C) 4224 D) 4884	2. D
3. 9 hours after 10:30 P.M. is 7:30 A.M. and 30 minutes later is 8 A.M. A) 11 A.M. B) 10 A.M. C) 9 A.M. D) 8 A.M.	3. D
4. $(200 - 100) \div (100 - 50) = 100 \div 50 = 2$. A) 2 B) 1 C) 0.5 D) 0	4. A
5. Choose the number in which "5" is the 4th place from the right. A) 3456 B) 34567 C) 345678 D) 3456789	5. C
6. $0 \div 1 = 0 = 1 \times 0$, so choice C is correct. A) $1 + 0$ B) $1 - 0$ C) 1×0 D) $\frac{1}{0}$	6. C
7. $2 = 14/7$; now, find the largest numerator. Choice B is largest. A) $\frac{11}{7}$ B) $\frac{17}{7}$ C) $\frac{15}{7}$ D) 2	7. B
8. One million $= 1000000$, so choice A is correct. A) 1000000 B) 100000 C) 10000 D) 1000	8. A
9. $100 = 10^2$, $400 = 20^2$, and $900 = 30^2$. A) 100 B) 200 C) 400 D) 900	9. B
10. $(1 \times 1985)+(2 \times 1985)+(3 \times 1985)+(4 \times 1985) = (1+2+3+4) \times 1985$. A) 10×1985 B) 12×1985 C) 24×1985 D) 25×1985	10. A
11. $30 = 2 \times 15 = 2 \times 3 \times 5$, so it has 3 prime factors. A) 0 B) 1 C) 2 D) 3	11. D
12. $\frac{1}{2} + \frac{2}{4} + \frac{3}{6} + \frac{4}{8} = \frac{1}{2} + \frac{1}{2} + \frac{1}{2} + \frac{1}{2} = 2$. A) $\frac{1}{2}$ B) $1\frac{7}{8}$ C) 2 D) $2\frac{1}{8}$	12. C
13. When a certain number is divided by 8, the quotient is 4 and the remainder is 0. The number is $8 \times 4 + 0 = 32$. A) 2 B) 12 C) 24 D) 32	13. D
14. From 5 degrees below zero to zero is an increase of 5 degrees. From zero to 5 degrees above zero is also an increase of 5 degrees. From 7 A.M. to 1 P.M., the temperature rose 10 degrees. A) 0 B) 5 C) 10 D) 25	14. C
15. For all choices except C, the sum of the digits is a multiple of 3. A) 27 B) 57 C) 77 D) 87	15. C

Go on to the next page ⫸ **E**

	Answers
16. $\frac{42}{16} = 42 \div 16 = 2\frac{10}{16} = 2\frac{5}{8}$. A) $2\frac{3}{8}$ B) $2\frac{1}{2}$ C) $2\frac{3}{4}$ D) $2\frac{5}{8}$	16. D
17. Multiples of 33 are 33, 66, 99, 132, ... 66 is a multiple of 22. A) 11 B) 44 C) 66 D) 132	17. C
18. $22 \times 33 \times 55 = 2 \times 11 \times 3 \times 11 \times 5 \times 11$, so choice B is correct. A) 1 B) 11 C) 5 D) $11 \times 11 \times 11$	18. B
19. There are 20 books on a shelf. If 12 books are removed, 12/20 = 60/100 = 0.60 = 60% were removed. A) 8% B) 12% C) 40% D) 60%	19. D
20. The cost of 4 shirts & 6 ties is \$84. 1 tie costs \$4, so 6 ties cost \$24 & 4 shirts cost \$84–\$24 = \$60. 1 shirt costs $\$60 \div 4$ = \$15. A) \$6 B) \$10 C) \$15 D) \$60	20. C
21. Value of the left-most "3" is 300 000 and value of the right-most "3" is 300. Since $300\,000 \div 300 = 1000$, choice B is correct. A) 300 B) 1000 C) 3000 D) 100 000	21. B
22. Since the two acute angles have a sum of 90°, larger one ≥ 45°. A) 40° B) 50° C) 88° D) 89°	22. A
23. Smallest factor greater than 1 is 5; largest one is $1985 \div 5 = 397$. A) 5 B) 397 C) 401 D) 1984	23. B
24. The first 10 words cost 40¢. The next 5 words cost 5×3¢ = 15¢. The total cost of a 15-word telegram is 40¢ + 15¢ = 55¢. A) 45¢ B) 55¢ C) 85¢ D) \$4.15	24. B
25. $3 \times 3 \times 3 \times 2 \times 2 = (3 \times 2) \times (3 \times 2) \times 3 = 6 \times 6 \times 3 = 6^2 \times 3$. A) $3^2 \times 2^3$ B) 9×4 C) $6^2 \times 3$ D) 27×8	25. C
26. A cat catches 7 mice in 4 days. Since 16 days = 4×4 days, it should catch 4×7 mice in 16 days. A) $4 \times 4 \times 4$ B) 4×7 C) $7+7$ D) 7×7	26. B
27. Product of prime factors of *any* number is the number itself. A) 10 B) 14 C) 35 D) 70	27. D
28. A car is driven at the rate of 30 km per hour. In 60 minutes it covers 30 km, so in 1 minute it covers $30 \div 60 = ½$ km. A) 15 km B) 2 km C) $\frac{1}{2}$ km D) 4 km	28. C
29. During the first 3 hours, the clerk addressed 140 + 120 + 170 = 430 letters. In order to average 150 letters per hour for the four-hour period, he must address a total of $4 \times 150 = 600$ letters. So, he needs to address 600 – 430 = 170 letters during the fourth hour. A) 130 B) 150 C) 160 D) 170	29. D

Go on to the next page ➡ **E**

30.	$0.1 = 0.10$, $0.1 \div 0.1 = 1.00$, $0.1 \times 0.1 = 0.01$, & $0.1 + 0.1 = 0.20$. A) 0.1 B) $0.1 \div 0.1$ C) 0.1×0.1 D) $0.1 + 0.1$	30. C
31.	By ratios, $85\% : 34$ questions $= (85\% \div 17) : (34$ questions $\div 17) =$ $5\% : 2$ questions $= 100\% : 40$ questions; so 100% is 40 questions. A) 50 B) 40 C) 38 D) 29	31. B
32.	The average is $99 \div 3 = 33$. Since one number is 34, the sum of the other two is 65. The other numbers are 32 and 33. A) 33 B) 32 C) 31 D) 1	32. B
33.	The distances between the 1st & 2nd, 2nd & 3rd, 3rd & 4th, 4th & 5th, 5th & 6th, 6th & 7th, 7th & 8th, 8th & 9th, and 9th & 10th are all 4 m. Since there are 9 distances, the total is 36 m. A) 36 m B) 40 m C) 44 m D) 80 m	33. A
34.	Product is 72 & difference is 71, so numbers are 72 & 1; sum is 73. A) 17 B) 27 C) 18 D) 73	34. D
35.	3^{100} is the only odd one since it's a power of an odd number. A) 2^{99} B) 3^{100} C) $(3+3)^3$ D) $(2+2+2)^2$	35. B
36.	The area of the shaded region is the difference in the areas of the two circles. Since Area $= \pi r^2$, the shaded area $= \pi \times 5^2$ $- \pi \times 2^2 = 25\pi - 4\pi = 21\pi$. A) 6π B) 9π C) 21π D) 29π	36. C
37.	Since $1^2 = 1$, $2^2 = 4$, $3^2 = 9$, . . . , $30^2 = 900$, $31^2 = 961$, and 32^2 $= 1024$, the squares are the 30 numbers 2^2, 3^2, 4^2, . . ., 30^2, & 31^2. A) 30 B) 31 C) 60 D) 499	37. A
38.	In a triangle, the sum of the lengths of 2 sides must be more than the 3rd. Since $4+7 < 12$, the perimeter cannot equal 23 cm. A) 23 cm B) 26 cm C) 30 cm D) 37 cm	38. A
39.	1234, 1243, 1324, 1342, 1423, 1432, 2134, 2143, 2314, 2341, 2413, 2431, 3124, 3142, 3214, 3241, 3412, 3421, 4123, 4132, 4213, 4231, 4312, 4321. A) 4 B) 12 C) 20 D) 24	39. D
40.	Had the distance been 600 km, it would have taken 2 hr to get there and 1 hr to return. Flying 1200 km in 3 hr averages 400 km/hr. In fact, *any distance* (600 km or not) gives an average speed of 400 km/hr, which is *not* ½(300+600) = 450 km/hr. A) 400 km/hr B) 450 km/hr C) 500 km/hr D) 550 km/hr	40. A

The end of the contest ✍ **E**

Solutions

1985-86 Elementary Grades Contest

for students in grades 5 & 6

E

Contest Information

- **Solutions** Turn the page for detailed contest solutions (written in the question boxes) and letter answers (written in the *Answers* column to the right of each question).

- **Scores** Please remember that *this is a contest, not a test*—and there is no "passing" or "failing" score. Few students score as high as 30 points (75% correct). Students with half that, 15 points, *deserve commendation!*

- **Answers & Rating Scale** Turn to page 88 for the letter answers to each question and the rating scale for this contest.

1. $(1986 - 1985) + (1984 - 1983) = 1 + 1 = 2.$
   A) 0 B) 1 C) 2 D) 1982

   1. C

2. Number of months in a year = 12, number of days in a week = 7, & number of minutes in an hour = 60. Sum is $12+7+60 = 79$.
   A) 77 B) 79 C) 1760 D) 1960

   2. B

3. $987 - 789 = 987 - 787 - 2 = 200 - 2 = 198.$
   A) 202 B) 192 C) 198 D) 208

   3. C

4. If John spends \$5.42 on groceries and \$7.29 on hardware, John spends all together \$5.42 + \$7.29 = \$12.71.
   A) \$12.61 B) \$12.71 C) \$12.81 D) \$12.91

   4. B

5. $5 + 5 + 5 + 5 + 5 + 5 + 5 + 5 + 5 + 5 = 10\times5 = 50.$
   A) 5 B) 45 C) 50 D) 55

   5. C

6. $(1\times9) + (2\times9) + (3\times9) + (4\times9) = (1+2+3+4)\times9 = 10\times9 = 90.$
   A) 89 B) 90 C) 99 D) 100

   6. B

7. $1986 + 1000 = 2986$, so add 1 to the digit 1.
   A) 1 B) 9 C) 8 D) 6

   7. A

8. $10 + (0\times10\times10\times10\times10) = 10 + 0 = 10.$
   A) 0 B) 10 C) 50 D) 20000

   8. B

9. 230 hundreds $= 230\times100 = 23000.$
   A) 23000 B) 2300 C) 230000 D) 23000000

   9. A

10. Since the factors in choice D are largest, their product is largest.
    A) 1983×1983 B) 1984×1985 C) 1985×1986 D) 1986×1987

    10. D

11. $5\times5\times5\times5 = 625 = 5^4$, so choice B is correct.
    A) 4^5 B) 5^4 C) 4×5 D) 5^5

    11. B

12. In an isosceles triangle, 2 angles have equal measures. If one has measure 20°, the other angles are *either* 20° & 140° *or* 80° & 80°.
    A) 20° B) 40° C) 60° D) 180°

    12. A

13. $\frac{1}{3} + \frac{1}{3} + \frac{1}{3} + \frac{1}{3} + \frac{1}{3} + \frac{1}{3} = \frac{6}{3} = 6\div3 = 2.$
    A) $\frac{6}{18}$ B) 1 C) 2 D) 3

    13. C

14. The sum of 1456366 and 1368444 must have a ones' digit of 0.
    A) 2824810 B) 2824812 C) 2824814 D) 2824816

    14. A

15. Since 19 and 21 are odd numbers differing by 2, their GCF is 1.
    A) 1 B) 2 C) 40 D) 19×21

    15. A

16. $4000 + 4000 = 8000 = 0 + 8000$, so choice A is correct.
    A) 0 B) 1 C) 2000 D) 8000

    16. A

Go on to the next page ⟶ **E**

17. If the plane had been 25 minutes late, it would have landed at 5 P.M. But it was 15 minutes later, so it landed at 5:15 P.M. A) 3:45 P.M. B) 3:50 P.M. C) 5:05 P.M. D) 5:15 P.M.	17. D
18. Since 21 = 3×7 and 22 = 2×11, the correct answer is choice C. A) 21 B) 22 C) 23 D) 24	18. C
19. Since the area of each square is 16, the side of each square is 4. The dimensions of the rectangle are 4 by 8 and its perimeter is 2×(4+8) = 24. A) 16 B) 24 C) 28 D) 32	19. B
20. 4000×2000 = 2000×4000, so choice C is correct. A) 8000 B) 6000 C) 4000 D) 1000	20. C
21. Since 9×9 = 81, the product of 9 and 12345679 ends in 1. A) 111111119 B) 111111118 C) 111111113 D) 111111111	21. D
22. My average cost per day was $600÷12 = $50. A) $720 B) $612 C) $50 D) $20	22. C
23. 2×3×4×5 = 4×5×(2×3) = 4×5×6. A) 6×8×10 B) 4×5×6 C) 4×6×10 D) 3×8×10	23. B
24. 1986 = 2×993 = 2×3×331, so choice C is correct. A) 993 B) 662 C) 331 D) 111	24. C
25. When a certain number is divided by 7, the quotient is 4 and the remainder is 3. This certain number is 4×7 + 3 = 31. A) 7 B) 19 C) 25 D) 31	25. D
26. Five children divided some cake equally. Two of the children together got 2/5 of the cake and 2/5 = 0.4 = 40%. A) 5% B) 10% C) 20% D) 40%	26. D
27. 24 hours = 24×60 = 1440 mins. 1440÷20 = 72, so I earned $72. A) $3 B) $8 C) $24 D) $72	27. D
28. 10% + 20% + 30% + 40% = 100% = 1.00. A) 1 B) 10 C) 100 D) 1000	28. A
29. The cost of one liter of cola is half the cost of one liter of juice. If juice costs $2 per liter, cola costs $1 per liter. The total cost of one liter of cola and one liter of juice is $2 + $1 = $3. A) $2 B) $3 C) $4 D) $6	29. B
30. Al types 2 pages less than Ann each minute, so Al will be 100 pages behind Ann in 100÷2 = 50 minutes. A) 50 B) 100 C) 200 D) 300	30. A

Go on to the next page ⅢⅢ➡ **E**

31. If the first and last digits of each of the numbers are interchanged, the new numbers are 5768, 5687, 5876, and 5678. A) 8765 B) 7685 C) 6875 D) 8675	31. D
32. Every 9 hours, the arrow points to 6. So, in 18 hours and 27 hours it points to 6. Since 24 hours is 3 hours before 27 hours, it points to the number that comes 3 numbers before 6. Thus, in 24 hours it points to 3. A) 2 B) 3 C) 6 D) 9	32. B
33. After 5 tests, average was 80, so sum of tests was $5 \times 80 = 400$. Average after 2 more grades were added was 76, so the sum of 7 tests is $7 \times 76 = 532$. His exam grade was $(532-400) \div 2 = 66$. A) 52 B) 66 C) 72 D) 76	33. B
34. The points are in the order A, C, and B. Distance from A to B is 15 cm and the distance from C to A is 8 cm. Distance from B to C is $15 - 8 = 7$ cm. $A\ \ 8\ \ C\ \ 7\ \ B$ A) 23 cm B) 20 cm C) 10 cm D) 7 cm	34. D
35. The difference between the two 4-digit numbers formed is $9861 - 1689 = 8172$. A) 8172 B) 8148 C) 7875 D) 4905	35. A
36. Clock shows the correct time after a 12-hr loss. With a 10-min. loss daily, it takes 6 days to lose 1 hr & 72 days to lose 12 hr. A) 36 days B) 72 days C) 120 days D) 144 days	36. B
37. For example, if a radius of the 1st circle is 2, a diameter of the 2nd one is 2 & its radius is 1. The ratio of areas is $2^2 : 1^2 = 4:1$. A) 4 to 1 B) 2 to 1 C) 1 to 2 D) 1 to 4	37. A
38. Bob earns \$11 every 2 days. To earn \$88, Bob needs to work a total of $8 \times 2 = 16$ days. So, he must work an additional 10 days. A) 10 B) 14 C) 16 D) 22	38. A
39. Choice D is approximately $(0.6 \times 60) \div 6 = 6$. A) $\dfrac{6.13 \times 5.89}{0.62}$ B) $\dfrac{61.3 \times 5.89}{0.62}$ C) $\dfrac{61.3 \times 5.89}{6.2}$ D) $\dfrac{0.613 \times 58.9}{6.2}$	39. D
40. The first perfect square is 1^2, the 2nd is 2^2, and the 3rd is 3^2. With this pattern, the 100th perfect square is $100^2 = 100 \times 100 = 10\,000$. A) 100 B) 1000 C) 10 000 D) 100 000	40. C

The end of the contest ✍ **E**

Solutions

1991-92 Annual 4th Grade Contest
Spring, 1992

4

Contest Information

■ **Solutions** Turn the page for detailed contest solutions (written in the question boxes) and letter answers (written in the *Answer Column* to the right of each question).

■ **Scores** Please remember that *this is a contest, not a test*—and there is no "passing" or "failing" score. Few students score as high as 24 points (80% correct). Students with half that, 12 points, *deserve commendation!*

■ **Answers & Rating Scale** Turn to page 89 for the letter answers to each question and the rating scale for this contest.

1991-92 4TH GRADE CONTEST SOLUTIONS

		Answer Column
1. The sum of *any* number of zeroes is 0. A) 0 B) 1 C) 10 D) 11		1. A
2. If, five years ago, I was 5 years old, then today I am 10 years old. Five years from now, I will be 15 years old. A) 10 B) 15 C) 20 D) 25		2. B
3. 1+2+3+4 = 11−10 + 12−10 + 13−10 + 14−10 = 11+12+13+14 − 40. A) 10 B) 15 C) 40 D) 50		3. C
4. Ten-thousand divided by two-thousand = 10 ÷ 2 = 5. A) 5 B) 20 C) 5000 D) 8000		4. A
5. 2 + 2 + 2 + 2 = 8 = 2×2×2. A) 2 B) 2×2 C) 2×2×2 D) 2×2×2×2		5. C
6. 7777 is *exactly* divisible by 7, so 7778 leaves a remainder of 1. A) 0 B) 1 C) 2 D) 8		6. B
7. Since 30 × 40 = 1200 and 3×4 = 12, 30×40 = 3×4×100. A) 0 B) 10 C) 100 D) 400		7. C
8. Add an odd and an even number to get an odd number. A) 51 + 51 B) 36 + 63 C) 12 + 24 D) 49 + 51		8. B
9. If I have three dozen pens, then I have 3×12 = 36 pens. A) 30 B) 36 C) 39 D) 42		9. B
10. 1 × 9 × 9 × 2 = 9×9×2 = 81×2 = 162. A) 21 B) 162 C) 180 D) 1992		10. B
11. The whole numbers less than 1000 are 0, 1, 2, 3, . . . , 999. A) 997 B) 998 C) 999 D) 1000		11. D
12. If today is Monday, every 7 days is another Monday. A) Monday B) Tuesday C) Friday D) Sunday		12. A

Go on to the next page ⅢⅢ➡ **4**

13. In the list of numbers 1, 2, 3, 4, 5, 6, 7, 8, 9, all the numbers in the list *except* 1 and 2 are exactly 2 more than some other number in the list. For example 6 is 2 more than 4. A) 2　　B) 7　　C) 9　　D) 11	13. B
14. If bubble gum costs 5¢ per piece, the number of pieces that Ali can buy for $2.00 is $200 \div 5 = 40$. A) 10　　B) 20　　C) 40　　D) 195	14. C
15. The number must be $51 \div 3 = 17$. A) 153　　B) 27　　C) 17　　D) 16	15. C
16. $(1993 - 1992) \div (1992 - 1991) = 1 \div 1 = 1$. A) 0　　B) 1　　C) 1991　　D) 1992	16. B
17. Since Jill is 2 cm taller than John, and John is 3 cm taller than Jim, Jill is 5 cm taller than Jim. A) 5 cm taller　　B) 5 cm shorter C) 1 cm taller　　D) 1 cm shorter	17. A
18. Since half of a year is 6 months, and 6 years is $6 \times 12 = 72$ months, six and one-half years $= 6 + 72 = 78$ months. A) 65　　B) 68　　C) 72　　D) 78	18. D
19. On a sheet of paper, a line is drawn through the center C of a square. As shown, this line intersects (or crosses) the square twice. A) 0　　B) 1　　C) 2　　D) 3	19. C
20. The product gets larger as the numbers get closer. A) 47×53　　B) 48×52　　C) 49×51　　D) 50×50	20. D
21. 16 minutes *before* 3:15 P.M. is 1 minute before 3:00 P.M. A) 2:59 P.M.　　B) 2:99 P.M.　　C) 3:59 P.M.　　D) 4:59 P.M.	21. A
22. $1234 + 5678 = 1200 + 30 + 4 + 5600 + 70 + 8 = 6800 + (30 + 70) + 8 + 4 = 6912$. A) 6666　　B) 6789　　C) 6912　　D) 7032	22. C

Go on to the next page ⟫ **4**

23. If I am going to retire when I am 65 years old, and that is 30 years from now, my present age is 65-30 = 35.

A) 20   B) 25   C) 30   D) 35

24. If special stamps cost 17¢ each, then 8 of these stamps cost 8×17¢ = 136¢ = $1.36.

A) 25¢   B) 56¢   C) $1.26   D) $1.36

25. (50-40)+(40-30)+(30-20)+(20-10)=10+10+10+10=40=50-10.

A) 50   B) 50 - 10   C) 50 + 10   D) 50 × 10

26. The *largest* 4-digit even number using these digits exactly once each ends in an 8 and is 9758. The tens' digit is 5.

A) 9   B) 8   C) 7   D) 5

27. When it's divided by 3, the quotient is 240. When divided by twice as much, 6, the quotient is half as large—it's 120.

A) 720   B) 480   C) 120   D) 80

28. The boy becomes 4 cm shorter each year. At age 10, he is 2 m = 200 cm tall. At age 25 years, he will have become 15×4 = 60 cm shorter. His height is then 200 cm - 60 cm = 140 cm.

A) 140 cm   B) 100 cm   C) 60 cm   D) 40 cm

29. If the 1000 whole numbers consist of 999 1's and the number 1000, their product will be 1000 and their sum will be 1999.

A) 1000   B) 1992   C) 1993   D) 1999

30. The perimeter of a small square is 4, so one "small side" is 1. Square *ABCD* has 8 "small sides" on its perimeter, so it has a perimeter of 8×1 = 8. (Don't count the "sides" *inside* square *ABCD*!)

A) 8   B) 12   C) 16   D) 20

The end of the contest 4

72

Solutions

1991-92 Annual 5th Grade Contest
Spring, 1992

5

Contest Information

- **Solutions** Turn the page for detailed contest solutions (written in the question boxes) and letter answers (written in the *Answer Column* to the right of each question).

- **Scores** Please remember that *this is a contest, not a test*—and there is no "passing" or "failing" score. Few students score as high as 24 points (80% correct). Students with half that, 12 points, *deserve commendation!*

- **Answers & Rating Scale** Turn to page 90 for the letter answers to each question and the rating scale for this contest.

1. $(1992 + 1992) \times (1992 - 1992) = (1992 + 1992) \times 0 = 0.$

   A) 0   B) 1   C) 1992   D) 3984

   1.
   A

2. $50+51$ is more than $50+50$, so $50+51$ is more than 100.

   A) 47 + 48   B) 50 + 51   C) 49 + 50   D) 48 + 49

   2.
   B

3. $703 + 307 = 700+300 + 3+7 = 1000 + 10 = 1010.$

   A) 110   B) 1010   C) 1100   D) 10010

   3.
   B

4. The product of the number of days in a week and the number of months in a year is $7 \times 12 = 84.$

   A) 5   B) 19   C) 60   D) 84

   4.
   D

5. $(11 + 22 + 33) \div (1 + 2 + 3) = 66 \div 6 = 11.$

   A) 10   B) 11   C) 30   D) 33

   5.
   B

6. The whole number factors of 4 are 1, 2, and 4. For 5, they're 1 and 5. For 9, they're 1, 3, and 9. For 8, they're 1, 2, 4, and 8.

   A) 4   B) 5   C) 8   D) 9

   6.
   C

7. Jack has seven dozen pencils and Jill has eight dozen pencils. Jill has one dozen more than Jack, and one dozen is 12.

   A) 1   B) 12   C) 24   D) 96

   7.
   B

8. Odd + even is odd, so $949 + 494$ won't have an even sum.

   A) 977 + 111   B) 282 + 828   C) 189 + 891   D) 949 + 494

   8.
   D

9. The sum of 7 numbers is 567. Their average is $567 \div 7 = 81.$

   A) 81   B) 88   C) 91   D) 98

   9.
   A

10. $11-10+12-10+13-10+14-10+15-10 = 11+12+13+14+15-50.$

    A) 10   B) 16   C) 50   D) 100

    10.
    C

11. Jan+Feb+Mar=31+(28 or 29)+31=90 or 91. Day 100 is in Apr.

    A) March   B) April   C) May   D) June

    11.
    B

Go on to the next page ⫸ **5**

1991-92 5TH GRADE CONTEST SOLUTIONS

12. $1\times2\times3\times4\times5\times6 = (1\times2)\times(3\times4)\times(5\times6) = 2\times12\times30.$

   A) 18   B) 20   C) 24   D) 30

13. Since 4 goes into 36 exactly 9 times, 37 will leave a remainder of 1 when divided by 4.

   A) 37   B) 35   C) 31   D) 27

14. $1 + 22 + 333 + 4444 = 23 + 333 + 4444 = 356 + 4444 = 4800.$

   A) 4790   B) 4800   C) 5000   D) 5100

15. I own 1 white, 2 black, and 3 brown pigs. The white pig is the *only* one which is *not* the same color as one or more of the other pigs, so it's the only one who could make that statement.

   A) 3   B) 4   C) 5   D) 6

16. Since one-half year is 6 months, and 9 years is $9\times12 = 108$ months, nine and one-half years $= 6 + 108 = 114$ months.

   A) 95   B) 104   C) 108   D) 114

17. The product $10\times10\times10\times10\times10\times10$ is $1\,000\,000$, and this number has 7 digits.

   A) 6   B) 7   C) 10   D) $1\,000\,000$

18. As shown, the line can intersect 0, 1 or 2 times.

   A) 3   B) 2   C) 1   D) 0

19. Ann *makes* 5 out of every 6 shots she tries. If she tries 30 times, it's like 5 rounds of 6 shots. She'll *make* $5\times5 = 25$ shots.

   A) 20   B) 24   C) 25   D) 29

20. One thousand thousands is equal to 1 million.

   A) 10×10 B) 100×100 C) 1000×100 D) 1000×1000

21. If he left at 7:20 A.M., he'd have 40 minutes to get to school on time. Leaving at 7:21 A.M. leaves 1 minute less than that.

   A) 21   B) 29   C) 39   D) 79

Go on to the next page ⁍ **5**

22. 300 and 15 are both divisible by 15, so 300+15 is divisible by 15.

A) 115   B) 215   C) 315   D) 415

22.

C

23. Any two consecutive whole numbers are 1 apart, so the difference between any two such numbers is always 1.

A) 1   B) 2   C) 996   D) 1992

23.

A

24. If two *different* whole numbers are both less than 10, they *could* be 0 and 1. In such a case, their product would equal $0 \times 1 = 0$.

A) 0   B) 1   C) 100   D) 101

24.

A

25. Divide out the common numbers. The number remaining is 27.

A) 1   B) 4   C) 5   D) 27

25.

D

26. The smallest odd number greater than 399 is 401. When 401 is divided by 10, the remainder is 1.

A) 0   B) 1   C) 3   D) 9

26.

B

27. In rectangle $ABCD$, the side *opposite* $\overline{BD}$ is the segment parallel to $\overline{BD}$.

A) $\overline{AB}$ B) $\overline{CD}$ C) $\overline{BC}$ D) $\overline{AC}$

27.

D

28. Every prime greater than 2 is odd, so its ones' digit is odd.

A) 1   B) 3   C) odd   D) even

28.

C

29. 3 gremlins = 5 gizmos; $3 \times 15 = 45$ gremlins $= 5 \times 15 = 75$ gizmos.

A) 27   B) 30   C) 47   D) 75

29.

D

30. A whole number is a *perfect square* if it is the product of two equal whole numbers. Thus, 1×1 and 2×2 and 3×3 and 4×4 are perfect squares. Continue until the product is bigger than 1000: $30 \times 30 = 900$; $31 \times 31 = 961$; $32 \times 32 = 1024$ (too big).

A) 30   B) 31   C) 32   D) 33

30.

B

The end of the contest 5

Solutions

1991-92 Annual 6th Grade Contest

Tuesday, March 10, 1992

6

Contest Information

- **Solutions** Turn the page for detailed contest solutions (written in the question boxes) and letter answers (written in the *Answers* column to the right of each question).

- **Scores** Please remember that *this is a contest, not a test*—and there is no "passing" or "failing" score. Few students score as high as 30 points (75% correct). Students with half that, 15 points, *deserve commendation!*

- **Answers & Rating Scale** Turn to page 91 for the letter answers to each question and the rating scale for this contest.

1. The only missing month is February. The sum will be either 365 – 28 or (in leap years) 366 – 29. *Both* are equal to 337. A) 334 B) 335 C) 336 D) 337	1. D
2. Since 5 divides 1000, 900, and 90, the remainder is 2. A) 1 B) 2 C) 3 D) 4	2. B
3. $(100-1)+(101-2)+(102-3)+(103-4) = 99+99+99+99 = 400-4.$ A) 0 B) 3 C) 4 D) 10	3. C
4. An even number has a factor of 2. Such a number, when multiplied by 5, will have a factor of 10. Its ones' digit will be 0. A) 0 B) 1 C) 2 D) 5	4. A
5. $10^3+(10^3-10^2)+(10^2-10)+(10-8) = 1000+900+90+2 = 1992.$ A) 2008 B) 2002 C) 1998 D) 1992	5. D
6. 400 – 100 = 300, and 300 is 50 less than 350. A) 350 B) 300 C) 200 D) 150	6. A
7. 5 nickels + 5 quarters = 25¢ + \$1.25 = \$1.50 = 15 dimes. A) 3 dimes B) 8 dimes C) 10 dimes D) 15 dimes	7. D
8. $7766-6677 = (7600-6600)+(100-77)+(66) = 1000+23+66 = 1089.$ A) 1089 B) 1099 C) 1189 D) 1199	8. A
9. The five whole number divisors of 16 are: 1, 2, 4, 8, and 16. A) 16 B) 34 C) 85 D) 121	9. A
10. When I divided by 2, it was as if I had only doubled my age, added 10, then subtracted twice my age. This leaves 10. A) 0 B) 5 C) 10 D) 20	10. C
11. 31 + 29 = 60; so, in a leap year, the 70th day will be March 10. A) 9th B) 10th C) 11th D) 12th	11. B
12. No prime larger than 6 can be a factor of $(1\times2\times3\times4\times5\times6)$. A) 7 B) 8 C) 9 D) 10	12. A
13. If *every* number is an 8, the average of *any* number of 8's is 8. A) 1 B) 8 C) 64 D) 88	13. B
14. Ten-million ÷ ten-thousand = 10 000 000÷10 000 = 1000. A) 10 B) 100 C) 1000 D) 10 000	14. C
15. 475 min = 8 hrs–5 min; so 1 P.M. + 8 hrs–5 min = 8:55 P.M. A) 7:55 P.M. B) 8:45 P.M. C) 8:55 P.M. D) 9:55 P.M.	15. C

Go on to the next page ⫸ **6**

78

16. $2^8-2^7-2^6-2^5 = 256-128-64-32 = 256-224 = 32 = 2^5$. A) 2^5　　　B) 2^4　　　C) 2^3　　　D) 2^2	16. A
17. Mark is 12 and his sister is 6. Their mother is twice the sum of their ages, so their mother's age is $2(12 + 6) = 2(18) = 36$. A) 18　　　B) 24　　　C) 32　　　D) 36	17. D
18. It's a geometric fact: the sum of the angles of a triangle is 180°. A) 180°　　　B) 120°　　　C) 90°　　　D) 60°	18. A
19. $7777 \div 7 = 1111$; $7777 \div 77 = 101$; $7777 \div 7777 = 1$. A) 7　　　B) 77　　　C) 777　　　D) 7777	19. C
20. 10% of 10% = 1/10 of 10% = 1%. If 1% is 2, then 100% is 200. A) 20　　　B) 100　　　C) 120　　　D) 200	20. D
21. If the shuttle circles the earth once every half-hour it circles the earth twice every hour, which is 48 times in 24 hours. A) 48　　　B) 36　　　C) 24　　　D) 12	21. A
22. Dividing 58 000 by 58, the quotient is 1000, with no remainder. Dividing 57 999 by 58, the quotient is 1 less than 1000; it's 999. A) 1　　　B) 9　　　C) 99　　　D) 999	22. D
23. The primes are 23 and 29, and their sum is $23 + 29 = 52$. A) 44　　　B) 50　　　C) 52　　　D) 54	23. C
24. $\sqrt{1} + \sqrt{4} + \sqrt{9} + \sqrt{16} = 1 + 2 + 3 + 4 = 10 = \sqrt{100}$. A) $\sqrt{10}$　　　B) $\sqrt{25}$　　　C) $\sqrt{30}$　　　D) $\sqrt{100}$	24. D
25. In a square, $p = 4s$, so a side is 1/4 (or 25%) of the perimeter. A) 4　　　B) 25　　　C) 40　　　D) 400	25. B
26. Any such whole number must have at least one digit different from 0. The sum of all of the digits of 100 or 1000 is 1. A) 0　　　B) 1　　　C) 2　　　D) 3	26. B
27. The choices other than 48 are not the *greatest* common factor. A) 4　　　B) 8　　　C) 12　　　D) 48	27. D
28. The *prime* factorization of 72 is $2 \times 2 \times 2 \times 3 \times 3 = 2^3 \times 3^2$. A) $2^2 \times 9$　　　B) $2^3 \times 9$　　　C) $2^3 \times 3^2$　　　D) $2^2 \times 3^2$	28. C
29. Sine $77 \times 888 = 7 \times 11 \times 8 \times 111$ and $88 \times 777 = 8 \times 11 \times 7 \times 111$, the ♦ can be replaced by =, since $(77 \times 888) = (88 \times 777)$. A) <　　　B) =　　　C) >　　　D) ≠	29. B
30. $0 = 0 \times 1$, $2 = 1 \times 2$, and $56 = 7 \times 8$. Only $63 = 7 \times 9$ *cannot* be expressed as the product of two consecutive whole numbers. A) 0　　　B) 2　　　C) 56　　　D) 63	30. D

Go on to the next page ⫸ **6**

31. Since each perimeter is 4, each side is 1. It would take 4 rows of 4 squares each, 16 in all, to cover the square with side 4. A) 1 B) 4 C) 8 D) 16	31. D
32. If the sum of five *different* positive integers is 500, the sum $1+2+3+4+490 = 500$ shows that the largest could be 490. A) 102 B) 490 C) 494 D) 499	32. B
33. Subtracting 6 from one of the numbers has the same effect as subtracting 1 from each of the six—so their average is 1 less. A) 6 B) 10 C) 11 D) 12	33. C
34. With 1992 numbers *all together*, the *number* of evens minus the *number* of odds must be even, so the difference cannot be 1111. Examples are 996–996=0; 1346–646 = 700; 1992–0 = 1992. A) 0 B) 700 C) 1111 D) 1992	34. C
35. A hexagon has 6 sides. Since the length of each side is a whole number, the perimeter of the hexagon must be greater than 5. A) 5 B) 1991 C) 1992 D) 1993	35. A
36. $3-2 = 1, 5-3 = 2$, and $11-3 = 8$. The difference cannot be 7. A) 1 B) 2 C) 7 D) 8	36. C
37. A circle and a square intersect as shown. Since a side of the square is 2, its area is 4. The *full* circle's area is $\pi r^2 = 4\pi$, so the quarter-circle is π, and shaded = $4-\pi$. A) $4\pi - 4$ B) $4 - \pi$ C) $2\pi - 4$ D) $\pi - 2$	37. B
38. The 2nd number exceeds the 1st by 4; the 3rd number exceeds the 1st by $4+4 = 2\times4$; the 4th number exceeds the 1st by $4+4+4 = 3\times4$. The 200th number exceeds the first by $199\times4 = 796$. A) 200 B) 796 C) 800 D) 804	38. B
39. The sum of the squares of the first 20 positive integers is 2870. The sum of the squares of the first 19 is $2870-20^2 = 2870-400$. A) 2350 B) 2361 C) 2470 D) 2850	39. C
40. My dog was 100 m from home, and my cat was 80 m from home. I called them, and they both ran directly home. If my dog ran twice as fast as my cat, my cat ran only 50 m when my dog ran 100 m; and the cat was $80-50 = 30$ m from home. A) 20 m B) 30 m C) 40 m D) 50 m	40. B

The end of the contest 🖑 **6**

Answer Keys & Difficulty Ratings

● ● ● ● ● ● ● ● ● ● ● ● ● ● ● ● ● ●

1979-80 through 1985-86

ANSWERS, 1979-80 CONTEST

1. C	9. A	17. D	25. D	33. D
2. B	10. B	18. B	26. C	34. C
3. C	11. D	19. C	27. D	35. A
4. D	12. D	20. B	28. B	36. D
5. C	13. B	21. C	29. B	37. A
6. A	14. C	22. B	30. C	38. B
7. A	15. A	23. A	31. B	39. C
8. C	16. A	24. B	32. D	40. D

RATE YOURSELF!!!
for the 1979-80 ELEMENTARY GRADES CONTEST

Score	Rating
36-40	Another Einstein
33-35	Mathematical Wizard
30-32	School Champion
27-29	Grade Level Champion
24-26	Best In The Class
21-23	Excellent Student
18-20	Good Student
14-17	Average Student
0-13	Better Luck Next Time

ANSWERS, 1980-81 CONTEST

1. C	9. A	17. C	25. B	33. B
2. B	10. D	18. B	26. B	34. A
3. C	11. A	19. C	27. D	35. D
4. A	12. A	20. D	28. D	36. C
5. B	13. B	21. C	29. C	37. C
6. D	14. A	22. D	30. B	38. C
7. C	15. C	23. A	31. B	39. B
8. D	16. D	24. A	32. A	40. C

RATE YOURSELF!!!
for the 1980-81 ELEMENTARY GRADES CONTEST

Score	Rating
38-40	Another Einstein
35-37	Mathematical Wizard
32-34	School Champion
28-31	Grade Level Champion
25-27	Best In The Class
22-24	Excellent Student
20-21	Good Student
17-19	Average Student
0-16	Better Luck Next Time

ANSWERS, 1981-82 CONTEST

1. A	9. D	17. B	25. B	33. C
2. A	10. B	18. D	26. C	34. C
3. C	11. C	19. C	27. B	35. B
4. B	12. B	20. A	28. D	36. A
5. A	13. A	21. C	29. B	37. B
6. D	14. B	22. B	30. D	38. D
7. A	15. B	23. A	31. B	39. C
8. D	16. C	24. D	32. D	40. C

RATE YOURSELF!!!
for the 1981-82 ELEMENTARY GRADES CONTEST

Score	Rating
38-40	Another Einstein
35-37	Mathematical Wizard
32-34	School Champion
29-31	Grade Level Champion
26-28	Best In The Class
23-25	Excellent Student
21-22	Good Student
18-20	Average Student
0-17	Better Luck Next Time

ANSWERS, 1982-83 CONTEST

1. A	9. B	17. D	25. B	33. A
2. D	10. C	18. C	26. B	34. C
3. B	11. D	19. D	27. C	35. C
4. A	12. B	20. B	28. A	36. A
5. C	13. C	21. D	29. B	37. B
6. B	14. B	22. B	30. A	38. B
7. B	15. D	23. B	31. D	39. B
8. D	16. B	24. D	32. D	40. A

RATE YOURSELF!!!
for the 1982-83 ELEMENTARY GRADES CONTEST

Score	Rating
37-40	Another Einstein
34-36	Mathematical Wizard
31-33	School Champion
28-30	Grade Level Champion
25-27	Best In The Class
22-24	Excellent Student
19-21	Good Student
16-18	Average Student
0-15	Better Luck Next Time

ANSWERS, 1983-84 CONTEST

1. D	9. C	17. B	25. D	33. C
2. D	10. B	18. C	26. D	34. C
3. A	11. A	19. C	27. A	35. A
4. B	12. C	20. B	28. C	36. B
5. C	13. B	21. A	29. A	37. D
6. B	14. B	22. C	30. B	38. B
7. A	15. A	23. C	31. A	39. A
8. C	16. B	24. C	32. B	40. D

RATE YOURSELF!!!
for the 1983-84 ELEMENTARY GRADES CONTEST

Score	Rating
36-40	Another Einstein
33-35	Mathematical Wizard
30-32	School Champion
27-29	Grade Level Champion
25-26	Best In The Class
22-24	Excellent Student
18-21	Good Student
14-17	Average Student
0-13	Better Luck Next Time

ANSWERS, 1984-85 CONTEST

1. B	9. B	17. C	25. C	33. A
2. D	10. A	18. B	26. B	34. D
3. D	11. D	19. D	27. D	35. B
4. A	12. C	20. C	28. C	36. C
5. C	13. D	21. B	29. D	37. A
6. C	14. C	22. A	30. C	38. A
7. B	15. C	23. B	31. B	39. D
8. A	16. D	24. B	32. B	40. A

RATE YOURSELF!!!
for the 1984-85 ELEMENTARY GRADES CONTEST

Score	Rating
36-40	Another Einstein
33-35	Mathematical Wizard
29-32	School Champion
26-28	Grade Level Champion
23-25	Best In The Class
20-22	Excellent Student
17-19	Good Student
14-16	Average Student
0-13	Better Luck Next Time

ANSWERS, 1985-86 CONTEST

1. C	9. A	17. D	25. D	33. B
2. B	10. D	18. C	26. D	34. D
3. C	11. B	19. B	27. D	35. A
4. B	12. A	20. C	28. A	36. B
5. C	13. C	21. D	29. B	37. A
6. B	14. A	22. C	30. A	38. A
7. A	15. A	23. B	31. D	39. D
8. B	16. A	24. C	32. B	40. C

RATE YOURSELF!!!
for the 1985-86 ELEMENTARY GRADES CONTEST

Score	Rating
39-40	Another Einstein
36-38	Mathematical Wizard
33-35	School Champion
30-32	Grade Level Champion
28-29	Best In The Class
25-27	Excellent Student
22-24	Good Student
19-21	Average Student
0-18	Better Luck Next Time

ANSWERS, 1991-92 4th Grade Contest

1. A	7. C	13. B	19. C	25. B
2. B	8. B	14. C	20. D	26. D
3. C	9. B	15. C	21. A	27. C
4. A	10. B	16. B	22. C	28. A
5. C	11. D	17. A	23. D	29. D
6. B	12. A	18. D	24. D	30. A

RATE YOURSELF!!!
for the 1991-92 4th GRADE CONTEST

Score		Rating
27-30		Another Einstein
24-26		Mathematical Wizard
22-23		School Champion
19-21		Grade Level Champion
17-18		Best In The Class
14-16		Excellent Student
11-13		Good Student
9-10		Average Student
0-8		Better Luck Next Time

ANSWERS, 1991-92 5th Grade Contest

1. A	7. B	13. A	19. C	25. D
2. B	8. D	14. B	20. D	26. B
3. B	9. A	15. C	21. C	27. D
4. D	10. C	16. D	22. C	28. C
5. B	11. B	17. B	23. A	29. D
6. C	12. D	18. A	24. A	30. B

RATE YOURSELF!!!
for the 1991-92 5th GRADE CONTEST

Score	Rating
27-30	Another Einstein
25-26	Mathematical Wizard
22-24	School Champion
20-21	Grade Level Champion
17-19	Best In The Class
15-16	Excellent Student
13-14	Good Student
10-12	Average Student
0-9	Better Luck Next Time

ANSWERS, 1991-92 6th Grade Contest

1. D	9. A	17. D	25. B	33. C
2. B	10. C	18. A	26. B	34. C
3. C	11. B	19. C	27. D	35. A
4. A	12. A	20. D	28. C	36. C
5. D	13. B	21. A	29. B	37. B
6. A	14. C	22. D	30. D	38. B
7. D	15. C	23. C	31. D	39. C
8. A	16. A	24. D	32. B	40. B

RATE YOURSELF!!!
for the 1991-92 6th GRADE CONTEST

Score	Rating
37-40	Another Einstein
34-36	Mathematical Wizard
30-33	School Champion
26-29	Grade Level Champion
24-25	Best In The Class
20-23	Excellent Student
17-19	Good Student
13-16	Average Student
0-12	Better Luck Next Time

93

Math League Contest Books
4th Grade Through High School Levels

Written by Steven R. Conrad and Daniel Flegler, recipients of President Reagan's 1985 Presidential Awards for Excellence in Mathematics Teaching, each book provides schools and students with:

- Easy-to-use format designed for a 30-minute period
- Problems ranging from straightforward to challenging
- Contests from 4th grade through high school

1-10 copies of any one book: $12.95 each ($16.95 Canadian)
11 or more copies of any one book: $9.95 each ($12.95 Canadian)

Use the form below (or a copy) to order your books

Name: _____

Address: _____

City: _____ State: _____ Zip: _____
(*or Province*)   (*or Postal Code*)

Available Titles	# of Copies	Cost
Math Contests—Grades 4, 5, 6		
Volume 1: 1979-80 through 1985-86	_____	_____
Volume 2: 1986-87 through 1990-91	_____	_____
Volume 3: 1991-92 through 1995-96	_____	_____
Math Contests—Grades 7 & 8		
Volume 1: 1977-78 through 1981-82	_____	_____
Volume 2: 1982-83 through 1990-91	_____	_____
Math Contests—7, 8, & Algebra Course 1		
Volume 3: 1991-92 through 1995-96	_____	_____
Math Contests—High School		
Volume 1: 1977-78 through 1981-82	_____	_____
Volume 2: 1982-83 through 1990-91	_____	_____
Volume 3: 1991-92 through 1995-96	_____	_____
Shipping and Handling		$3.00

Please allow 4-6 weeks for delivery Total: $_____

MasterCard
□ Check or Purchase Order Enclosed; **or**
□ Visa / MasterCard # _____
VISA
□ Exp. Date_____ Signature _____

Mail your order with payment to:
Math League Press
P.O. Box 720
Tenafly, NJ USA 07670

Phone: (201) 568-6328 • Fax: (201) 816-0125

94